CW01065235

# EVOLVE

Rebecca Robertson

Evolve
Copyright © 2016 Rebecca Robertson. All rights reserved.
First paperback edition printed 2016 in the UK
ISBN 978-1-910815-16-8

A catalogue record for this book is available from the British Library.

No part of this book shall be reproduced, stored or transmitted in any form or by any means, electronic or mechanical, including photocopying, recording, or by any information retrieval system without written permission of the publisher.

Published by Herkimer Publishing
www.HerkimerPublishing.com

Design by CMB Designs
www.cmbdesigns.co.uk

Printed in United Kingdom

Although every precaution has been taken in the preparation of this book, the publisher and author assume no responsibility for errors or omissions. Neither is any liability assumed for damages resulting from the use of the information contained herein.

# Praise

"I loved reading this book. It's not often you get a fabulous financial advisor helping you look at the practicalities of managing money AND deal with the inner games, thought and beliefs which challenge us. If you're looking for a practical, step by step way to become financially free then look no further. I love the exercises and simple ways you can start managing your money and creating greater wealth. A fab read for every woman wanting to take better control of her wealth."
– Yvette Taylor Creator of EAM – The Energy Alignment Method™
www.yvette-taylor.com

"This is a brilliant book, and should be recommended reading for every woman! A mix of personal experience, psychology and education, it's easy (and enjoyable) to read and packed with important financial insights, practical exercises, and wisdom. It delves into your personal relationship with money, and helps you to identify and unpick any bad habits – and develop a healthier, more liberating relationship with money. It's a comprehensive, yet common sense, approach to finance that you'll reap the rewards from for the rest of your life."
– Hannah Martin – Co-Founder Talented Ladies Club
www.talentedladiesclub.com

"If you want to understand money and plan for your future but not sure how to go about it, then I highly recommend you start reading Rebecca's book today. I've taken away so much from reading it and have used it to form my own financial goals and how to achieve them. Rebecca is an expert in her field, the feedback from her clients is 5* and I know from my own personal dealings with her she is an expert in her field of financial management for women. I recommend this book to you and know it will give the confidence and motivation to use your money wisely and create the future you want."
– Jane Ollis, Kent Chairman Institute of Directors
www.quvium.co.uk

"Rebecca's no nonsense approach to helping women with their finances is refreshing. The combination of Rebecca's story, the psychology behind money mind set and how to practically tackle your finances to allow them to blossom is empowering. A fabulous read. Highly recommended."
- Liz Almond, Small Business Mentor - Money Mind set specialist
www.insightfulminds.co.uk

"What I love about Evolve is the linking of psychology to the financial principles that one needs to master to thrive financially. Through sharing personal stories and simplifying the process with useful exercises, this book creates an opportunity for many women to recognise their financial behaviours and reasons for managing money the way they do. I'm a firm believer that financial education for women is essential, so am delighted to see this book available in the marketplace to address women's financial empowerment."
-Laura Morrison, The Game Changer Consultancy
www.thegamechangerconsultancy.com

"One of the greatest challenges facing women (and men for that matter) is that we are not taught about money. At best we learn to make it, but rarely to manage or grow our wealth. With practical exercises and simple explanations this great book goes a long way to overcoming this problem. Her back to basics approach will do financially overwhelmed women and their families, world of good."
-Dr Joanna Martin
www.joannamartin.com

"Whatever your money situation right now, this book holds precious gems and long-awaited answers to your money questions.
Rebecca Robertson is on a mission to empower women when it comes to money - equipping them with the essential information, understanding and tools to improve financial health, build financial wealth and ultimately create the sort of financial security and freedom that is life changing.
Whatever your own financial goals and aspirations, developing your financial health and wealth with the sort of insights and know-how contained in this book, is an important element of becoming fully empowered."
-Nicola Huelin Founder of Mpower Mastermind Groups for Mums in Business'
www.mpower.global

'I am a real advocate of empowering women and Rebecca's book will further this cause. It is a practical approach to ditching some limiting beliefs that may be holding you back and helps you evolve into someone who takes control and makes savvy financial decisions. One third of Mums in the UK earn the same or more than their partner. These female breadwinners will continue to increase and will find this book invaluable. I recommend it for all smart women."
-Jenny Garrett Award Winning Executive Coach, Author of Rocking Your Role
www.JennyGarrett.Global

"Thank you Rebecca, I thoroughly enjoyed reading EVOLVE. The insight you offer is timely and specifically catered for those whom perhaps, like yourself initially, were unable to comprehend the complexities of finances. I totally agreed with the points you made re-education of finance being key, I also enjoyed the context within which you placed the book, it always helps to picture the author and their journey to being the expert that you have clearly become. The emotional complexities surrounding money and our attitude towards the same is also useful; how we behave with money and certainly our attitude towards debt is also I believe that which we were taught as acceptable by our parents. As a single parent myself I had to check myself over the rationality versus one's wish list argument! And finally the appreciation of shoes was extremely insightful! Super reading, LADIES need and should read EVOLVE!
- Camilla Choudhury - Khawaja LL.B Hons LL.M BVC The Women's Lawyer
www.thewomenslawyer.co.uk

"I loved Rebecca's book.  She explained everything simply and with ease; a true sign of a professional in their field.  Her exercises really got me thinking and planning my way to a more secure wealth building future.  This book is a must read for every woman.  The more knowledge we learn on how to handle our own finances the more empowered we become and the greater our influence becomes on the female generations younger than us."
- Star Monroe
www.star-monroe.com

# Contents

# CHAPTER 1
## Why the focus on women?

I am happily married and was brought up by my dad as a single parent, so I have nothing against men. In fact, the complete opposite. They are both my rocks and have helped me get to where I am today. This is often a misunderstanding, it's as though; if you like watching football you won't like watching rugby. When, in reality, you simply have a passion for football. It isn't about exclusion but equality.

For me, working in a male dominated industry for many years, I was trained by managers who were men, compliance checked by male supervisors and monitored by male managers. Without knowing, I mimicked their mannerisms and their way of doing things. I became, like a lot of women in the industry, institutionalised. I was often the only female adviser and certainly the only female manager with or without adviser experience. The women in the office were administrators. The environment didn't encourage them or new starters to progress. The industry has a reputation of being pushy and at times selling to clients, not always putting the clients first, which I've experienced first-hand. Many women don't feel comfortable working in this kind of environment and they aren't encouraged to progress either. Consequently, 90% of financial planner/mortgage brokers are men. I don't include bank staff as they are tied agents and, unless they get established in an independent firm before they have a family, the opportunity becomes less likely.

For these reasons, I believe women haven't felt they can trust the industry as a whole to get independent or 'whole of market' advice. Research has revealed that women are less likely than men to seek professional financial advice across all areas of finances, with only 7% of women taking professional advice to help them plan for retirement compared to 16% of men. Furthermore, 34% of women who have not sought financial advice say they would never seek professional financial advice, and only 12% say they plan to seek advice in the future.

Imagine if schools provided financial education and then families, particularly women, followed it up with home education. Would students get into less debt? Would those in their mid-twenties make different financial decisions? I believe so.

Women in the past have tended to pass the financial decisions over to their partners to deal with. However, we are finding more couples are making decisions together or the female is holding the purse strings and, therefore, wanting to make educated financial decisions. Women have every reason to make sure their financial future is secure. They tend to have gaps in employment after looking after their children, meaning many will have a reduced pensionable income. But women are living longer and surviving their partners, they often have jobs that are based on their passion not how much they earn, they are more generous in nature (not putting their financial needs first but their family's wants) and, generally speaking, they are less likely to take risks with their money.

I am noticing an amazing wave of women in business and in senior roles that is so positive. These women are wanting more for themselves and their future. We have directives on how many women are at board room level and, in Theresa May, Britain has a second female Prime Minster.

I hope you will join us in this journey and evolution for women.

# CHAPTER 2
## My Evolve Story

The purpose of writing this book at the outset was purely to help more clients and be able to support existing clients with more information around money management. As with most situations, it didn't stay this way. As time went by, more people encouraged me to write my own story. Because it was my own money story, which was just as important as my original message, I fought this for quite some time, saying it wasn't about me, it was about the clients I was helping. This wasn't the 'Becky show'. I loved my business and what the brand stood for, but I hid behind it, much like most women. We step back and don't push ourselves into roles or positions that would be beneficial to us. We accept where we are, believing that's what we deserve to be. Even when we are encouraged and supported to make a leap, we still step back and don't feel as if we deserve or are worthy of the role/position. Why? What is it in our make-up that we can't see it for ourselves? I know women who have the full ability and potential but virtually sabotage themselves along the way, just to prove that they were right in the first place. We deserve more. We should demand more. Why not? We all have the right and the skill to achieve whatever we wish. We just have to believe it and grasp it with both hands.

Of course, there is the other side to the coin where the women who do this are seen as money grabbing or a 'bitch'. It might be the green-eyed monster, but I also feel that the way women are portrayed in films and cartoons does have an influencing factor. Take Cruella de Vil, she has money, drives a flash fast car and has a large house but she is the villain. There are many more examples. Women are portrayed as either the businesswomen with no children and, therefore, so career-minded that there is no time for anything else in her life, or the mother figure at home who cooks fresh meals every day and waves her children off at the school gates. We are so much more than either of these people. If either were to become successful in their own right, often the individual would be considered a hard-nose person with no emotion in the decisions made – just as men are expected to be strong, make business-like decisions and have no emotion in their conviction. It is time we, male and female, let go of these stereotypes and stand in the space we believe belongs to us while showing others they can do the same.

So I have sat here nervously writing out my thoughts in hope it will help others and with the belief in my heart that I deserve my spotlight as much as the next person. Is it because I am a millionaire, or that I have a perfect life, or that I know everything and couldn't learn anymore? No, I am none of these things. If we all waited until we were in the perfect position, no one would achieve anything. We would just see others flying ahead of us and we would be left wondering when it is our time.

It often surprises people who know me that I was brought up by my dad as a single parent. They hear me speak about women's challenges, how women need more support and encouragement. In fact, I was raised in a male environment, my dad being a real man's man. My passion for the female cause, comes from my own experiences and those of the tribe of women I have around me. I see many more women needing financial assistance and less sure of where to start or turn. My female focus comes from my feeling that we haven't even seen the start of what we can achieve. My father was always a strong character and force in my childhood. He comes from a generation where you work hard, pay your bills and go to the pub on a Friday after work. As an industrial engineer, he got his hands dirty and worked long hours. His dad was in the Second World War and worked in the mines, his mum worked in a sewing machine factory, what was the true British working class. He saw those in high-level roles as people who went to university and were born with a silver spoon in their mouth. From his view point, there were limits, you couldn't be anything you wanted. You couldn't live the life of your dreams. He encouraged me to work hard, do my best and maybe I would get my own house with a mortgage and have a good job to pay the bills. His advice has actually done me well and given me a strong work ethic, I love and respect him very much. But for a long time, I believed that we all have limits and high levels of wealth were only for those from another social status.

At primary school, I wasn't classed as an academic. Who was I to disagree? I sat next to people who would help me maybe more than they should. Looking at my own strong-willed daughter now, I probably didn't help myself much. My memories of homework or learning from home was my nan trying to do spellings with me and getting so frustrated with me, likewise my dad helping me with fractions. I just didn't get it. There were little expectations for me to aspire to be something or someone. When it came to going to secondary school, they considered holding me back for a year, allowing me time to catch up. They decided to keep me with my friends and emotionally that was the best thing for me. When starting secondary school, they didn't know what do with me. I didn't have any special needs but I wasn't main stream. At that time, a few years ago now, they didn't have special schools for children. So they placed all those pupils who were below the bar into one class. As I sat in that room, I remember looking around wondering what I'd done to deserve to be there. The work they gave me was too easy and I knew that I needed to work harder to get ahead and back to the classes with my friends. It was the first moment in my life when I knew that I deserved better and that I was the only one who would make it happen. After a year, I was up in main stream and in English I was in the high set. With maths, however, I was still playing catch up.

When it came to choosing careers, I wanted to be a vet. The careers' teacher looked at me and suggested maybe becoming a hairdresser. I was the least 'girly' person ever. Brought up by my dad, older grandparents and having an older brother, I was a tom-boy. When out playing with friends, all boys, I was picked to play football third or fourth not last. I was one of the lads. My dad being a single parent with a family of five to support (including my grandparents) he didn't take me clothes shopping but instead I wore my brother's old tracksuits. Once, my mum bought for my birthday a pair of the latest Reebok trainers with an air bubble. I wore them into the ground. Something my dad would never be able to afford or buy. This was one of my first financial lessons. My mum was married to someone who worked within local government in a senior role. They had a large cottage in a pretty village, shopped in John Lewis and Marks & Spencer, whereas I lived in an ex council property and there was little spare money for any extravagances. It was two different worlds.

So back to my career choice. My family didn't think being a hairdresser was the right choice either. However, they explained becoming a vet meant having to acquire several GCSE's, five or more A Levels before six years-plus at university. They didn't believe it would be right for me or that I would be able to achieve it. After this, I didn't know what I wanted to do. I took my GCSE's achieving a few, nothing to be that proud of. A very similar story to other people's experiences.

I see the teenagers of friends being put under too much pressure when it comes to qualifications, which are important, of course, however they do cause stress at such a young age. What we are, in effect, teaching them is that to be successful you have to have these exams and you won't be successful without them. That is neither true nor right.

At 15, I left school and the only job I could do was strawberry picking. I got on my bike and rode it out to the fields, several miles away from home. I think I ate more strawberries than I picked in the first few weeks. Starting college at 16, to pay for my train fare, I worked in KFC and in factories fruit packing until midnight. I resented the fact that my family didn't pay for me, but this was my second financial lesson: only I could obtain money and no one was going to give it to me.

Fast forward a couple of years, I had gained a NVQ in Business at college and started working in office junior type roles. The first was as a filing clerk for a distribution company where I had thousands of pink and yellow slips to place in 30 cabinets. At 19, I was made redundant from a long-standing receptionist role. I found myself working in the Job Centre as a temp, helping others to find employment. Well, those who were interested. After three months, I was on my last working day, a Friday, thinking I would be signing on myself on the Monday. I had a phone call from an agency asking if I wanted a job the following day. What office is open on a Saturday, I thought. I told them my days of working in factories and KFC were over. They explained that it was working in a bank. My little head couldn't imagine me working in a bank. That was for those who went to university and were clever with maths. I had only just got my dad to open a bank account for me. I knew nothing about finances or money.

The next day, I went to work and saw a queue outside the bank at 8:30am. Getting in the building, I was taken downstairs to the staff kitchen area where on the table were hundreds of leaflets. They contained details of all kinds of 'terms of conditions' and types of accounts. I didn't know the difference between an easy-saver and a bond . . . or what an overdraft was. Within half an hour, a group of us was up on the bank counter with thousands of pounds of cash in the drawers next to us. The doors opened and people came in filling up the bank.

Now this wouldn't happen in this day and age. The branch was so short staffed, all the team on that Saturday were temps apart from a manager. I had never handled more than £200 before, let alone counting through large wads of notes in front of strangers. I was so nervous. Who in their right mind would want me working for them in a bank? The thing was, though, I was actually really good at it. The counting got easier with practice and I loved chatting to new people on the counter. Within three months, I was head cashier and was taken on permanently.

This is a picture of me with my uniform on and name badge, a proud moment for myself.

That is where my own career, my financial journey, started. However, my financial story had only just started. One day travelling to work, I had a car accident. My old VW polo was crushed in half from behind on an icy day by a driver not looking at the road. My car was spun around, leaving me feeling like a test dummy. The contents of the Polo were scattered all over the road. Thankfully, I escaped with just bad whiplash, but in those days you were sent on your way with little help. It took many years before my body was aligned and I could walk feeling straight and even. In the meantime, I took pain-killers to help with the terrible headaches.

During this time, I also met a boy, like you do, and we moved in together. Instead of saving to buy the furniture we needed, we took out an Argos store card. Sofas, tables, TV and bed, everything you would need to live comfortably. This was manageable but my spending continued with a car loan, after all my old car had been written off. It didn't stop there. I justified my extravagance to myself as I was earning good money and could afford the monthly payments. The credit card debt started to build up as I brought lovely shoes and clothes. I wasn't buying cheap and cheerful but top-of-the-line leather coats and handbags. Looking back, the reason I did this was to make myself feel better. I was in pain from my car accident and I enjoyed that initial buzz from having a lovely new pair of shoes. Having my hair done with a new outfit made me feel better, if only for a short while. But that was okay as I could go shopping again in a few days. I see women doing this at all ages a lot, not realising that they are doing it. Happiness cannot come from a new pair of shoes but from making others happy.

I partied every weekend, meals out and dancing to the early hours. We went on to buy our first flat for £118,000 in south-east London. My early twenties were a lot of fun. Even though I worked in a bank, this didn't give me an education around money. I was taught to sell products, as are bank staff to this day. I knew what saving was and how it worked and I knew how loans and credit cards worked, I sold all these products for the bank. I woke up one day and realised it had gone too far and I had built up nearly £20,000 in debt without the mortgage.

In this time, I had continued to work on my career and moved on to be an independent mortgage broker, earning good money for my age. I was promoted to a technical role in London and then was head hunted into another mortgage brokerage firm, working my way up the ladder to become a team leader. The commission was getting better – and the more hours I put in, the more I earned. I was able to reduce the debt to a manageable level by using as much as possible of my commission to pay off the credit cards, just leaving my car loan outstanding. The boy I'd moved in with had become my fiancé and we started to plan our wedding. This time, instead of paying for it using credit cards, I knew we had to save the money. We did just that. We paid for our wedding ourselves and our honeymoon to Disney, Las Vegas and New York. We had to make adjustments to our spending and make do with what we had. I had learnt to stop spending on credit cards and brought things when I had the money to do so. Simple but a massive mind-shift that was not easy.

While working in London and having this fantastic career, I didn't realise at the time that I had become institutionalised by the industry. It was, and still is, a very male dominated environment. I wore a shirt, I say that now and it sounds so weird, a T M Lewin shirt with cuff links. CUFF LINKS. I sometimes matched it with a pin-striped suit. Okay, this might be the 'thing to do' in London for men. The blacker the suit and the whiter the stripe the better. But for a 25-year-old female? What was I thinking? The team were aged 35-plus men and the management team were the same but older. It was such an environment that I didn't see how masculine it was, I became part of it. The way we were trained to speak to clients and recommend products was masculine. It was a fast and furious working place and, though the industry has calmed a little, the same training and practices are in place. I drew the line when one of the directors told me to go out to the sales floor, I was a sales manager at the time, take away an adviser's chair and "have a go" in front of everyone. The same director used to take advisers' chairs away from them if they didn't make enough calls a day and come with a massive golf umbrella, slamming it on the top and shouting: "Do more, do more quickly." I knew it was time to move on.

For a long time, I had tried to fit in, to be one of lads. But this wasn't as life was back when I was young . . . being picked to play football. This was my adult life and it should have been on my terms. I continued to use the ethics my dad had taught me, which was work hard and do your best, not realising that actually my best had reached a strong level. I was always pushing myself to do more or prove I was worth being listened to and that my opinion mattered.

Moving into my next role, still within financial services as a regional sales manager, the same ethos existed but there was a slightly nicer environment, and I was based from home. I enjoyed the diversity of the job and training new staff. My husband and I found out we were going to have our first baby. My manager at the time asked me to wait until I had to legally inform them and not before. I didn't understand what he was hinting at or why he was acting in such a way, only later to find out that redundancies were on the cards for the company. However, I had read up on my rights and knew I have more rights if I told them, so at 14 weeks I officially informed them I was pregnant. But at 15 weeks, I was made redundant along with the other regional manager, therefore I had no legal position in terms of being pregnant as I wasn't being discriminated against.

I was shocked and disappointed, I didn't know what the future held. But I took it in my stride, hoping for a new opportunity elsewhere. As my bump grew and I was looking for opportunities, the reality of my situation sank in. Who wanted to employ a pregnant women? I got in contact with past colleagues and discovered the industry wasn't doing so well in general, there was little contracting work or employed work.

After my daughter was born in 2008, the recession was officially announced and no one was taking on any work. Thousands of mortgage brokers and IFA's left the industry as business dried up. I started to apply for jobs outside the sector, looking for something different. Maybe something new that I had not come across before. I applied for what seemed like hundreds of jobs, in the end signing on the dole. The humbling experience of the Job Centre, from the other side of the counter, is not something I would like to repeat ever again. I took a folder with me and a copy of all the jobs I'd applied for along with follow-up notes. The staff didn't know what to do with me. Did you know you cannot take an umbrella into the main area in case you attack the staff with it? You have to leave it with security. I felt my career was over. My identity had been taken away. All those years of hard work for nothing. Many mums choose to stay at home and they thrive on it, enjoying every moment and wanting to do it with more children. But this wasn't the route I wanted to go down. I loved my time with my daughter but found the days long and missed my work purpose. I believed I could do both, but I had no idea how. I also wanted my own money and independence. I didn't want my husband paying for me. I saw too many women puzzling what to do next when their children became teenagers. Many felt they had missed out.

My family encouraged me to "go back and work in a bank", back to my roots. A couple of banks locally were looking for staff and I managed to get a job interview at one. Expecting an online or computer-based technical interview and a face-to-face conversation, I was shocked to be presented at the first stage of interviews with an off-the-cuff mathematical test. My baby brain was still popping up whenever it wasn't needed and, of course, at this interview. This is a real thing, ladies, I used to think it was me, but it really is. A friend of mine who is a brain surgeon confirmed that our brains shrink in pregnancy. I was given a piece of paper and pencil to make notes and I was asked: "A client comes into the bank with 20 £20 notes, 15 £5 notes and 12 bags of £1 coins, he wants to deposit the money into his account and take out £276 using only £20 notes and some light change, how much would be left in his account if they had a balance starting at £75?" I had a minute to give an answer while the person was sitting watching what I wrote and worked out. Anyone would have struggled. But because of the place I was in at the time, I took it as a personal failure. After all, I had worked at a senior level in a bank and more senior roles elsewhere. A cashier in a bank was going back several steps and I couldn't do it. After four questions, I stopped the interview and walked home crying.

We all have those moments where we feel like it couldn't get any lower. That was one. My husband, the ever supportive, told me not to worry and everything would be okay. But I couldn't see it. It was like I was under water and I couldn't hear what was being said, though I heard the tone being empathic and supportive. I wasn't able to take it on board.

After six months of signing on, I applied for a part-time, 14 hours office administrator role for a charity. I got an interview, which amazed me as most people so far had not considered me even for an interview, mainly as I was over qualified. I got the job and it was perfect for me to rebuild my skills and confidence. I kept my head down and did my work and went home. It wasn't the dream role and it didn't fulfil my soul but it gave me purpose and focus . . . and a belief that I was worth something. I appreciated that. After a year, I had found my feet and was more involved with the charity. I would have happily become their fund-raising person as I was great at drumming up interest and it was for a charity but there wasn't a role for me doing that. The administration role became repetitive, sending out the same letters for the same things week in week out.

Then, my old boss asked if I wanted to join a team he was putting together of insurance brokers. It was one of those defining moments where it could all go very right or very wrong. I turned him down a few times, still not confident enough to get back into the saddle. But in the end, I went for it. I knew that I wouldn't be content at the charity long term and that I'd tried most other industries, getting nowhere. It was time to take that leap. To push myself, if I wanted more. The first few months I was like a duck out of water, everything feeling familiar but I was not as clear or confident as before when it seemed like something I did with my eyes closed. Self-doubt kicked in often. The love of working back with clients, however, was brilliant and easy. I went to people's homes and had a chat with them about their family, about what concerned them. I felt valued like I was doing something worthwhile again. It is an amazing thing, when you find something you believe in and you are appreciated for it. All the money in the world cannot pay that.

Unfortunately, the team was closed down but I was invited to join the main company unit, doing what I was already doing but adding mortgages to it, which obviously was my thing from a long time previously. Again I thrived, but something wasn't right. I loved the job and I was paid well for it. What more could I ask for? But I couldn't sleep at night. I would lie awake feeling that something wasn't right. The firm I worked for, self-employed, would micro manage everyone, expecting 30-page client documents back into the office by 10am the next day, when you had seen the client only the night before. I would watch my little girl playing on the carpet whilst I had to get these reports done, feeling such guilt and anger as it just wasn't necessary to be managed in such a way. The situation went against everything I felt was right when it came to working WITH people, that collaboration and team work were key, not pushing to get the results you wanted. On top of this, I would be questioned on why certain products were "sold" to clients. Now firstly I don't feel any product is sold to anyone, there is a need and if it is needed then the client has the option to take the recommendation. However, certain firms will have key indicators that are used from a sales perspective just to ensure they are getting the maximum revenue, without any real consideration for the client's needs. It reminded me of my time back in London and the industry as a whole.

I was left wondering again what my next move was going to be. I had tried other job applications in different industries and I knew the way I did things was appreciated by clients. Why should I leave the industry and start again because I couldn't find a home to work in? Herein lies why so many women leave the financial services especially adviser-type firms and roles. If they aren't already established in their own right, they won't have the confidence to do this once they have children, often even without having children. I wasn't going to accept second best any longer. I wasn't going accept it was just how it was. Institutionalised or not, I wanted things done on my terms with how I wanted to work with advisers and with my clients. From somewhere, I found the strength to believe that I could do it myself. That if anyone was going to make a difference and stand for something positive, it was going to be me. I had done it for other firms . . . so why not for myself?

Yet if I thought I'd had a journey before and a story to tell, as we all have, starting a business was, along with being a parent, the biggest challenge I ever undertaken.

When I stood as a candidate for the London Assembly, representing the Women's Equality Party, I would never have guessed that it would lead to me meeting someone like Rebecca Robertson. We shared the same passion for empowering women in their careers and businesses and I had the privilege of speaking at the re-launch of her business network, 'Evo Girls'. Since then, I've been amazed at her drive, enthusiasm and dedication to helping women gain financial knowledge and skills. This book is the current step in a series of steps that Rebecca has taken through social media and other means to get her message across. However, 'Evolve' gives her the chance to tell her story in depth. What's great is that Rebecca has lived through most of the life scenarios she discusses in the book and, even better, has made lots of mistakes - big ones and little ones - which makes her an author who walks with the reader on their journey, rather than one who lectures from the side lines. As a barrister, I deal with a huge range of casework affecting women, ranging from employment law rights to custody disputes to financial claims and I am really glad that Rebecca has written this book to support these women in taking back control of their lives, not only financially, but holistically. As Rebecca says in this book, "I believe that it's not that women need extra help. They need different help." I couldn't agree more!

Isabelle Parasram

Founder of Leading Women International | former London Assembly Candidate for the Women's Equality Party | Head of Greycoat Law
www.isabelleparasram.com

# CHAPTER 3
## My Entrepreneur evolve story

The summer of 2011 is when I officially started my own business, launching with just a few friends and family at a working men's club with a short presentation on financial planning. The evening was a success so two months later I did another event, however I didn't know any more people than I did previously so I had the same crowd come along and only a few additions. It cost me money with food and drinks but it was enjoyable. In between these events, I paid to spend a couple of days at Orpington Shopping Centre being one of those annoying people who approach you when you are not interested even if you were giving away gold. I learnt a lot but that venue didn't work and I found the process and effort not rewarding. If you do not love doing it or you are not buzzing from it, what's the point? It wasn't that it wasn't a good idea just that it didn't get results, and therefore why I didn't enjoy it.

The following month I found myself networking. I started picking up ideas about email marketing so I created a MailChimp account to email people regularly. In the January, I found myself at a psychic fair where amazingly I did get some leads. But I was learning that I wasn't hitting my target market. I was also going to ladies' pamper events, and on my stand I had a lovely pamper basket to win in a prize draw. I had lots of people enter and I was getting some leads from it. But again, I felt as if the amount of work and effort wasn't being rewarded. It wasn't coming together in the way I had hoped. The same went for wedding shows. I thought I'd be hitting a target market there, but my timing was off. The couples were interested only in the fancy parts of getting married, few took the financial planning element seriously.

I went back to where I started and I ran another event called 'Empowering women networking'. My friends had grown bored of my 'business' by now and I found the new people supporting me were other businesswomen. Ten or so people came but again it cost me money to put on the event with little return, I couldn't spend another month promoting it and spending out money on it when it wasn't producing anything new... apart from the networking element.

We were now heading for Easter 2012 and I was using social media more and more, and the list was getting longer and more daunting. LinkedIn, a Facebook page and profile groups such as Pinterest, Twitter and WordPress as well as blogs, website and SEO. I continued to try out these different platforms to see which worked and which were too time-consuming. I was also drilling down into my market more and stopped attending wedding fairs and such like and was focusing on the new baby market, attending larger events in Kent and local smaller events in Medway. At some of these, I was getting 250-plus email addresses. However, after a year of working this marketing and attending events, obtaining more than 700 email addresses, I realised timing is key. If you are in your target marketing when their buying time is off, it's pointless. I still communicate with all those people via my MailChimp newsletter.

I continued to focus on the baby market, getting busier and busier, opening up a small office space in the September as my daughter had started school. I took the networking and the idea of the events, by creating Evo Girls, a support group for business working, not so much networking. We met once a month, and still do. In the January 2013, I took on an apprentice and everything was going really well. I didn't think so at the time, but you never do. You are just hoping and dreaming about pushing the business forward.

In the June, the new baby market went quiet and I was all out of ideas. Well, I wasn't, I had tons of them but I was tired. I didn't want to start another project. Then the kids were having the end of school fairs and things became even quieter. What should I do? Act, that's what. I started listing myself in directories where I didn't want to be before.

I really had to push myself to start another project. Being me, I didn't start one, I started four, one of which is a money make-over. I've been presenting a ladies networking event and enjoying the opportunity to help people with any questions or issues they may have.

In January 2014, I set myself the task to grow the business further and I launched my recruitment event for April in London with the plan for the new team to join in the September. It was a big step and outside my comfort zone. I set about organising contracts, manuals and processes. It took over my summer but was proud of the end result. I had a 30-plus index full of the knowledge I'd learnt over my 14 years' experience, now 16 years.

The team started and I continued to run the business, manage the team plus work with clients. It was stressful but the core business purpose was to create more jobs for women in financial services, therefore giving more women financial advice. It meant everything to me to make it work. A year on and the ladies had grown individually and in their skills.

Jennie Delelis has been a massive support to the business and is a great asset to the team. With Nadine Monks, we have created a specialist sister brand Evolution Forces Families - female financial planners working with the Armed Forces community, which Nadine has grown.

The year 2015 was the most challenging yet, due to processes and procedures. I set about creating a new client management system or client journey process. It turned my business upside down, which I knew would be challenging, but I underestimated the amount of new information I needed to take and absorb to get the project off the ground. It was a step backwards to make a leap forward.

We now have improved the client's journey with automated updates from head office - ensuring our clients are kept up to date continually. Our client files, emails and information are stored in one central record. This allows us, as advisers, to work closely with our clients and understand their needs even more. This has gone on to create a client charter, detailing our turnaround times and client aims as a team. High customer service standards are at the core of the business and why I am so proud to have won the Customer Service category at Kent Women in Business Awards 2015. In the past five years, I've been shortlisted, runner up to 12 other awards. But winning the Customer Service honour was an amazing feeling. One to remember.

- Kent Women in Business 2016 – Women in Finance. Shortlisted

- Kent Women in Business 2016 – Customer Service Award. Shortlisted

- Professional Adviser 2016 – Personality of the Year. Shortlisted (out of 35,000 advisers plus nationally)

- Corporate Live Wire 2016 Innovation & Excellence Awards. Won Excellence in Financial Advisory Services for Women Award

- Kent Women in Business 2015 - Won Customer Service Award

- Kent Women in Business 2016 – Leadership and Management. Shortlisted

- Corporate Live Wire 2015 Innovation & Excellence awards - Shortlisted

- Kent Independent Traders Awards 2014 - Finalist 'Professional Business

- Kent Women in Business – Small Business Owner of the year 2014 - Runner Up

- Kent Independent Traders Awards 2013 - Finalist Business Growth

- Kent Independent Traders Awards 2013 - Runner up Customer Services

- Women in Finance/banking – 2012 Jo Cameron's Achievers Academy for Women

I had managed to turn a concept that the industry and most people didn't really understand into a successful business with a team of advisers who are growing in their own ways. The ripple effect has been amazing to experience.

My next challenge was having a second child with a business, as if being a business owner wasn't crazy enough. But we cannot live in fear of what scares us. I won't allow other people's mind-sets to hold me back. We must give things a try and learn. That is growth . . . and Evolving.

So that's My Evolve Story. I hope to help more clients with their own financial journey and to create more opportunities for women to join the team and grow their own business, which will help more women with their finances. I firmly believe that the more women who feel empowered and confident with their money, the more this will pass on to their children. This is Evolution for Women.

Find out more about our journey here

http://evolutionforwomen.co.uk/rebecca-robertson-professional-speaker/

# CHAPTER 4
## Why women behave differently with money to men?

A recent survey carried out by the CII, The Chartered Insurance Institute, found that women say they do not understand some financial products enough in order to put their hard-earned cash towards them. As a result, they feel less confident about making financial decisions than men do. Women have so far tended to place their money into products such as current accounts or cash ISAs instead of more complex investment plans usually chosen by men.

### Why is there this lack of understanding?
History tells us that women have taken the back seat when it comes to family finances. Only once the Married Women's Property Acts of 1870 onwards which gradually over a period of 23 years gave women the rights to own assets independently.

It seems to be a culture that has remained and women have taken time to realise the fact that they need to know just as much as men about the family finances. More and more women are finding out that they don't know what to do when their spouse passes away and have been the subject of unlawful or incorrect advice as they don't know what is right or wrong.

The media have often stated that this is down to women not being interested in finance because it's boring and worrying, but do we really believe this? Or is it down to a very male dominated industry offering financial products that are targeted, let's face it, at men because they are created by men and have a male dominated thought process in them.

The current financial offerings are marketed as products, with a lot of jargon associated with them, and are advertised from a male point of view. This does not attract women, who want to know exactly what they are buying into in plain English from a person they can relate to so they can put a frame of reference around it.

I often hear clients saying to me that they have got advice elsewhere already but felt the process was rushed, that things weren't explained carefully and that they didn't feel they could ask questions.

## Looking inside their heads...

Money is a very emotionally loaded discussion and it drives more couples apart than other issues. Psychotherapist Olivia Mellon has done much research into this topic and has come up with some useful insights.

She mentions that money is inextricably linked with power, happiness, security, control, dependency, independence, freedom and love.  So, if someone has an issue with money, to talk about it brings up an awful lot of other problems that are in their subconscious.  This can evoke some really deep seated emotions.  To talk about money in a relationship can bring about a lot of guilt and anxiety, which can stop the conversations happening.  In turn, the problems don't go away and can often get worse.

Olivia Mellon says that men are brought up to see the world as competitive and hierarchical, there is always someone above you and someone below, however women see the world as co-operative and democratic, therefore sharing. Women are also encouraged to be seen as needy and vulnerable while men are discouraged from such behaviour.

When seeing clients, there are usually two roles taken by men, either "I'll pretend I am listening although I know this is important but 'she' (partner) can deal with this" or "I'll have a final say on this, I need to make sure I am protecting my family".  However in reality, if the partner has strong enough opinions then the man is often swayed towards her way of thinking.

This is different from when I first started my career, more than 15 years ago, where I was either speaking to the male or the female, often the male. Women have taken over making financial decisions around the household bills and food shopping due to procedures nowadays. In 65% of households, in fact, women are making those financial decisions. Men have, therefore, started to step away from the day-to-day decisions. Unfortunately, it has meant that some families haven't then received financial advice (which isn't on a comparison website). The new age of female financial consumer is still Evolving, she is independent and wants to understand the full spectrum of advice and make an informed decision.

## So why are female financial advisers a good idea?

In research, women have stated that they are put off from dealing with financial advisers because of the jargon that is put out in the media and negative stories that friends, family and the press have put forward. So, they miss out on potentially crucial information that could improve their financial situation.

There are many women who prefer to deal with a female financial adviser as they are discussing their very personal details because all the personal finance is always linked to lifestyle choices and family situations.

Unfortunately as a high percentage of advisers are men, it has given clients the impression that some of them do not have the client's best interest at heart. There are some amazing male advisers in the industry, who don't deserve this judgment. The impression has already been made, therefore the client is looking for an ear to listen to them and for them to feel they aren't going to be made to feel silly or incompetent in some way. Female advisers may give an impression of caring and nurturing clients, wanting to listen to their needs and allowing clients the time to make decisions without pressure.

## So why bother?

Women, in general, have more commitments and challenges within their lives than ever before. They tend to be the gender that juggles with parents, children, households and jobs/businesses. It's not surprising that they actually do need different financial advice than men. It is also vital that they see finance as an important part of their lives and something that they need to know and understand fully.

After all, women live longer than men, so need to provide for themselves for longer. Ironically, women earn less than men over a lifetime because of career breaks to have children, husbands posted abroad or elderly parents to look after.

According to the Centre for Economic and Business Research, it is predicted that by 2025 women will own 60% of the nation's personal wealth. It said women currently owned 48% of Britain's personal assets but this would rise to 60% by 2025 as women reaped the dividend of better qualifications, more equal pay, higher levels of home ownership and longer life expectancy. The research, carried out for the Liverpool Victoria friendly society, found there were already 47,355 female millionaires between 18 and 44, compared with 37,935 men.

Women are achieving better qualifications than men at GCSE and A-level. More women than men go on to higher and further education.

When women move into employment, they still encounter gender discrimination. Gross hourly earnings are 83% of the male average, compared with 63% in 1970.

"Given the increasing levels of education, success amongst women - coupled with the changes in mix of professions - this is expected to rise to at least 90% by 2025," Liverpool Victoria said.

Nearly two-thirds of women aged 20 to 24 live away from their parents, compared with 44% of men. Single women are more likely than single men to own their own home and are well placed to benefit from increasing property prices. Women who marry are likely to outlive their husbands, so wives are more likely to inherit their husbands' wealth than vice versa. Women live on average until 81, while male life expectancy is 76.6 years.

A Liverpool Victoria spokeswoman said: "This change will come about due to the rise of a cohort of financially sophisticated younger women, adding to the traditional sources of female wealth such as marriage and inheritance."

But women are less likely than men to make long-term financial plans or start a stakeholder pension. The friendly society said single women were much less likely to have mortgage protection, employment protection or permanent health insurance.

# CHAPTER 5
## Money blocks

### Why do we have blocks about money?

Most research states that money blocks stem from our early days. Maybe a parent has said that "money is the root of all evil" and that "being rich is selfish".  These beliefs can be instilled in you without you even being aware, and then throughout your life, you find yourself being without money because of an unconscious fear of having it.

A lot of financial advisers tell you that in order to be prosperous you need to make sure that you own your own home, pay off your debts, keep savings and, if you want to be a millionaire, run your own business. However as much as we read this, many people have no luck at making their millions and instead waste money on get-rich-quick schemes or the lottery without success.  So, why is that?

As I said before, it could be a belief that has been passed to you by your parents.  You are holding this as your own belief and using it to confirm that what you believe is correct when you are actually holding a losing ticket every week.

### How do we break down those blocks?

Becoming aware of our beliefs about money is a start. Breaking the connection between your parents' money blocks and your own is also necessary.  Try to find out what these blocks are . . . because once you do, you will be in a better position to consciously change your beliefs around money to more positive ones such as, "there is more than enough money to go around", or "I can enjoy money and still save for the future at the same time".

Here are some crucial questions to ask yourself to find out your inner most beliefs around money. You can also do this exercise with a personal friend or a business friend:

- What is your most painful money memory?
- What is your most joyful money memory?
- How did these experiences shape how you use money now?
- What three things did your parents teach you about money?
- When growing up, was your family, rich, poor or middle class?
- What were your family's values around money?
- What is your greatest financial fear?
- What are your most important financial goals?
- What are you willing to do differently around money?

Beliefs and ideas about money can also be attributed to personality. There are many different traits and these can be directly linked to a person's attitude towards money.

## What does our personality contribute to our beliefs about money?

There has been a large scientific study carried out in the UK to find out about personality traits and how they affect a person's relationship with money. It gives a simple yet effective explanation about our relationship with money for the vast majority of us.

The research was called the BBC's Big Money Test, which was a survey conducted on more than 100,000 people in 2015 by Professor Adrian Furnham from University College London, Professor Mark Fenton-O'Creevy from the Open University and BBC Lab UK. Its aim was to find out how personality affected attitudes to money and how relationships with money affected the risk of going into debt.

Firstly the research established that there are four distinct ways people view money. These have been labelled as Status Spender; Generous Indulger; Secure Saver; and Independence Lover. I will explain each of these shortly.

It determined that our relationship with money can, and does, affect the risk of being in trouble financially. So depending on which personality type you fall into can affect the risk level of getting into debt. There were other factors that affected our relationship with money and these are:

- ❖ A person's age was a big factor. It seems that young adults were at the bottom of the pile when looking at money management, mainly because they were not thinking about the future.

- ❖ Gender is also important to mention because women and men in general see money in a very different way. Women are more likely to spend more yet were more worried about how much they were spending than men. Men were more likely to see money as their route to freedom or as an achievement of their goals. Studies have also shown that women in general donate more to charity and will give money to their children before spending it on themselves.

The study then revealed that there are times when we are susceptible to thinking about money in wasteful ways . . . such as worrying all the time about how much we are spending, denying that we buy unnecessary things and retail therapy; buying things to make us feel better.

So, going back to the four different ways people view money and how it affects their spending, here is a summary of each:

Status Spender
Money means power to these people and they will usually be the type of people who will have the latest gadgets or drive the flashiest cars and will most likely buy everyone a drink in the pub or buy their friends dinner. These people are the most likely to have problems with personal relationships and could end up with large financial debt.

These type of clients will be approaching us about clearing debts and how they can get their head above water. However often once they have done this, they haven't looked at why they have been spending as they have been... What has made them feel that they need these 'status' items.

## Generous Indulger

These people love to buy gifts for their family and friends. They enjoy giving to the extent that it replaces genuine affection, according to psychologists, and they can have difficulty with their children as they get older because their children expect gifts all the time and more money to be spent on them at every opportunity.

I see a lot of women with children lavishly spending fortunes on their new babies, enough clothes for an African village, and their spending gets out of control, it makes them feel like they are taking care of their child better by purchasing these items. Often, I see their partner concerned about their spending and not understanding why they feel the need to do it. Once that habit has started, it is hard to change. It can extend into the children as they become older with the endless list of toys and higher end clothes, etc.

## Secure Saver

Money is security to these people and they feel better when they put it in the bank or into some kind of savings even when they don't need to save it. These people can end up denying themselves and their loved ones opportunities that could improve their financial situation because they are unwilling to take the risk.

I met a lady who had £35,000 sitting in an ISA, she kept the money separate from her family's monthly outgoings and savings and took great comfort that the money was there in case of emergency. To her, the idea of moving it or touching it was crazy.

## Independence Lover

Getting away from it all with holidays or taking sabbaticals are what these people crave. They use money to break free from the burden of everyday life. The important thing for this type to remember is that they need to look at other financial aspects of life, such as preparing for the unexpected events, for example ill health.

I have a client who really doesn't care how much she spends, not on little things, but holidays and summer holidays . . . and she will want to re-mortgage and take equity out her house to facilitate this. Her belief is that life is short after all and the money is there to spend.

So which one are you? Where do you sit within these habits?

## Written by Yvette Taylor creator of EAM

One really simple way to change your money blocks is a technique call The Energy Alignment Method (EAM).

EAM ™ is a powerful personal development tool. Designed to enable you to quickly change your thoughts, beliefs, memories, patterns, emotions and behaviours so you can feel more positive, happier and in flow (about anything not just money).

It is very common for people to experience feelings of stress, anxiety, worry, overwhelm and uncertainty when they think about money. The truth is focusing on money in this way only brings more negativity, which is usually creates the exact opposite of the thing you want.

Many personal development and law of attraction methods talk about having a positive mind set, doing meditations and affirmations. Whilst this IS essential, there is often one thing missing. How do you ACTUALLY let go of the things in your way?

With EAM we address both, with 5 simple steps you can transform what is standing in your way. This means you feel happier, more confident and able to think more positively about anything which is troubling you.

## THE 5 Steps to EAM

The process works by tuning into what is happening in your energy. You can do this by using a method from Applied Kinesiology known as "the sway". This process is a muscle and energy testing technique which gives us an ideomotor response. Which put simply is a YES or NO response from your body in answer to a question?

Before you begin (and when you're using this for the first time) we need to ensure that your YES and your NO are the right way around.

Stand with your feet hips width apart and relax your knees and your hips. Close your eyes.

Check you are aligned by something like "My name is (Say your name)" and notice if your body gentle sways forwards or backwards. You can check this with other simple question like "my date of birth is ...." Or "My middle name is ...." Etc. usually your sway forwards is a YES and backwards is a NO, sometimes it can be something else, but that takes more explanation.

Now you know your YES and your NO – you can ask your body simple yes/ no questions.

Think about something which may have been troubling you. Stand with your feet hips width apart, close your eyes and relax your knees.

## STEP 1 – YOU ASK
Example: Am I holding any resistance or worry when I think about making more money?"

## STEP 2 – YOU MOVE
Your energy body will respond and give you the YES or NO answer to the question you asked

Your Body Will Sway Forwards (YES) or Backwards (No)

## STEP 3 – YOU EXPERIENCE
There are 3 ways to complete this step but for this example just pay attention to how it makes you FEEL when you think about making more money.

Does it give you a tightness in your tummy or chest, heaviness in your legs? Just describe the physical sensations in your body.

## Step 4 – YOU TRANSFORM

Now you're clear what it feels like in your body – in this example perhaps tightness in your chest when you think about it. You can say these words.

*"I am ready to release (whatever the subject)* **this tightness in my chest when I think about making more money***. I release it from my energy in all forms, on all levels at all points in time"*

Repeat this statement at least 3 times or until you can no longer feel it. You may have do this another 2 or 3 times. Check in with the sway again and ask

*"Have I released this tightness in my chest when I think about money?"*

If YES then you can move to step 5. Do not move to step 5 until you have released the resistance around it.

## STEP 5 – YOU MANIFEST

Now you're ready to allow a new belief, thought or pattern. This time you get to choose what you experience in this case we want to have a better relationship with making more money. This is where you manifest your new future. It can be an emotion, belief thought, experience or anything you want to create.

Choose a positive affirmative statement

*"I am ready to receive/ create / feel / manifest/ experience "(whatever the subject)*

*e.g.* **Myself to feel happy and excited about making more money.** *I allow this into my energy energy, in all forms, on all levels, at all points in time."*

You should repeat this statement at least 3 times or until your body responds with a positive sway forwards (YES) when you are affirming. Keep repeating this statement until you feel it in your energy.

If you want to find out more about EAM and how to use it to shift your money blocks visit here http://www.energyalignmentmethod.com/freegiftevolve/ to download a short programme to introduce you to the 5 steps of EAM and a list of 88 common limiting beliefs around money and new ones you can install to start transforming your relationship with money.

# CHAPTER 6
## Financial intelligence

Unless you have studied finance at college or university, it is unlikely that you would class yourself as financially intelligent. Many women, therefore, avoid financial matters as they feel they aren't clever enough or understand them well enough.

IQ, that is intelligence quotient, is a total score derived from one of several standardised tests designed to assess human intelligence. So unless you have taken financial exams or you have cracked it personally with self-education, you wouldn't class yourself as financially intelligent.

Most women make decisions based on their emotions, Emotional Intelligence (EI). This is the capacity of individuals to recognise their own and other people's emotions, to discriminate between different feelings and label them appropriately. They use EI to guide thinking and behaviour, and to manage and/or adjust emotions to adapt environments or achieve their goal(s).

This is why so many female clients want to understand the full spectrum of information, not just the top three or four facts. This can

be misunderstood for questioning an expert but it is, in fact, how we process the information to then make an informed decision based on how they feel about it. Women tend to avoid these decisions if they do not understand all the facts. If they do make a decision often it can be something they regret or question later.

Women ask many questions of themselves when making financial decisions, such as:

They are taking into account not just their own position but they are wanting to know all elements are taken into account such as: affording it; what about the cover we have in place; what about what work may do for me; what about the investments we have already and what kind of return will that provide; is that enough, what about the children; what about our other goals; what will it stop us from achieving elsewhere?

When receiving financial advice, any good financial planner should ensure that you are taken through the process and your journey should be smooth. All these questions should be answered. Unfortunately, too many planners are focusing on particular products or areas of expertise and they are not discussing all the needs from a holistic position.

Regulated financial advisers/planners are regulated – so if the advice isn't right, you can be compensated for that. It is important to watch out for those giving advice in a non-regulated environment. They may have the best intentions and may not mean to give bad advice, but what is right for them isn't necessarily right for you.

Therefore, financial intelligence doesn't come naturally to anyone, you have to learn it and develop the skills to understand it.

Reading books
Sounds simple but a lot of people don't believe that they have time to read self-help books or believe that they won't help them. There are many great books out there aimed at helping you to improve their financial knowledge in a simple and practical way. Reading this book is a start, check out Amazon for other literature on finances, property, investments and the stock market.

Conferences
These are a great way to gather ideas and to meet with like-minded people striving for the same success. It's a good idea to look at the detail instead of the 'fluff' of the marketing material. Many have titles such as 'Become a millionaire in a Year', however in reality, there is no simple 'get rich quick' scheme.

Check out in the internet
There is a wealth of information online . . . from the latest financial news; YouTube with its 'How To' guides; and most importantly mind-set videos helping you progress and move forward.

# CHAPTER 7
## Money Makeover Programme ™

This programme has been put together after many years' experience working with clients. The process is the one I have always taken clients back to and asked them to look over again, as their feelings and thoughts don't change around it but the habits they seem to create do. Consistency in your approach is vital.

Our Money Makeover goes through five stages to help you change the way you feel about money and in order to assist you in using it to your advantage. The five steps are: analyse, assess, compare, budget and plan.

We will look at how to give yourself a financial detox and start fresh with a new plan and a new commitment to improving your financial wellbeing. The first stage is:

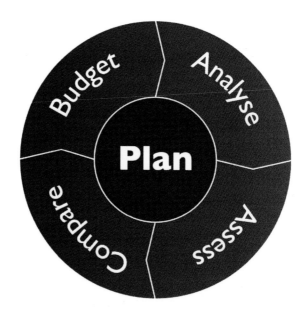

These exercises are best undertaken when you are in a quiet place with a note book, something to refer back to.

To analyse your beliefs about money, take a moment to read these sayings:-

"Money means nothing to me"

"Money means everything to me"

"Money is anything"

What does money mean to you? Do you feel that it means very little and how much you have in your bank account is no motivation at all? How long do you spend looking after your money – do you ignore it and put statements in the drawer?

Or do you love money? Do you look at your bank statements or online apps every day? Watch every penny?

Or is it that money gives you the ability to purchase certain items that makes you happy? New shoes or another dress? Maybe you like to spend money on others, such as family?

Or is money everything to you? Do you love it so much that you collect it under the mattress or in a bank account?

Or is money a facilitator to enable you to live a life of your choosing?

Money isn't always the physical amount, it can be the time we take out of the working day to help others, or it might mean giving to charity.

To me, money is grease, like putting oil on the wheels of a bike. It allows us to live a certain life and provide us with the tools to be comfortable now and in the future.

## What do you believe about money?
Going back to my Evolve Story, I described my childhood as having two financial elements, one of my dad's and one of my mum's, both having

different life-styles. Holidays were a good example. My dad would take us camping and we would drive to France, whereas my mum would fly abroad and stay in nice hotels.

I would like you to think about your childhood memories, where did your family take you on holiday? What did your parents do over the school summer holidays? What did your parents do with their money? Did they have a love or hate relationship with it?

We weren't taught at school about 'how to manage our finances', we learned from our family. We learned from their approach to money. Did your parents give you money without any questions? Did your mum or dad put money in the bank or under the mattress? Did they have a large property or more than one property? Your subconscious acts due to these past memories. We act in our early working years based on the past, either in a positive or negative manner. We continued our self-education after making mistakes and trying to rectify those mistakes.

I used to feel that I didn't deserve nice things; that they were for other people. Even now, as I spend money on renovating my house, not buying cheap and cheerful but buying high quality to ensure it lasts, often meaning it's more expensive. When we stop to think, we realise that such thoughts and decisions are our own limiting beliefs. We have inherited them. These thoughts have created habits that we might not even be aware of.

To help you become more aware of these potential habits, start making a note of some of the things we have mentioned. Do you look at the bank statements? Do you check your balance before you buy something? When was the last time you treated yourself? Some people put up Post-it notes around the house to help to remind them.

Once you start to know the answers to these questions, you will become more aware of how you feel about money. Are you a money hater or a money lover?

Like anyone wanting to change a bad habit – such as smoking or drinking too much - you first have to become aware of the problem. This is a great start, but without action there is little point. This is when we become disheartened. There are several books and techniques that can help you change your mind-set and help you assess these thought patterns in more detail and, therefore, find ways to make quick easy changes.

Clients who have had the best results have had certain things in common. First, if you don't have any clear goal or a determination to change, the likelihood of the change staying long term is very low. I sat with a couple where she was sure her partner wouldn't make any changes to enable them to carry out their house extension, meaning they would incur new monthly mortgage payments. For a year, they had been in a stand-off with both avoiding the subject. He wasn't wanting to be forced into giving up the little treats he allowed himself and the family. Their joint credit card was always needing clearing down, which she was doing with the savings she made each month. You see the cycle.

By following some of the exercises later in this programme, we were able to find middle ground and a compromise. What was frustrating was that they both had the same goal and the motivation . . . but the 'how' was the major obstacle. Exactly what adjustments were they going to make to their existing habits? With this couple, one small sticking-point was how much he spent on lunches. Hundreds of pounds were being laid out in McDonald's and coffee shops every month. And yet they were not able to go on a skiing holiday as they couldn't afford it. We changed the habit. His wife was more than happy to add his lunch needs to those of the children and, though it would cost her more, it would save the family overall . . . as then he could contribute more. The habit of going out to purchase lunch was taken away.

This pattern of 'lacking' is what I see all the time with clients. They feel they can't afford a holiday, a new car or to move house, etc. However, they spend money on things they can't even remember.

Usually men who like gadgets will justify unnecessary products claiming they NEED them when, in fact, they don't need them but they WANT them. This a huge difference.

In reality, many clients do not know where anything from £200 to £1200 a month is spent. This is due to failing to have any identification with their money. They just spend it. Having a goal, something you can identify with emotionally or even physically, is the most practical way to change this situation.

When do we stop and analyse where we are with our finances? After a year and looking back and wanting more? Inheriting money from a family member and spending it within a few months but can't account for what you spend the money on? When we lose our job and have to take a lower paid one? When we separate from our partner and our house money is halved? There are any number of milestones.

If we analysed more often, would our finances be in a better position? I think so.

## Exercise 1
This first exercise is designed to help you analyse your beliefs about money.

So many people dream of winning the Lottery, although I've read a number of stories about millions being wasted and not looked after properly. But just imagine you won £150,000. Imagine what you could do with it. Buy that new car, take the family on holiday and put in the new kitchen.

Firstly, write a list of six things, in order of priority, that you would spend the winnings on? Take your time, really think about it. What would you do with all that money? Once you have written these, think about the following questions:

◆ What does the list tell you about yourself?

◆ Have you spent the money on yourself or on someone else?

◆ Have you invested it or have you spent it on nice things?

What do the results tell you about your beliefs? Let me help you with this.

MONEY ACTIONS GRAPH

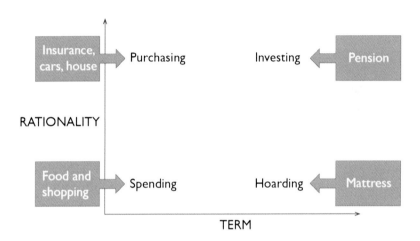

Along the bottom, we have the term of a purchase and along the side the rationality in the spending. We usually have four reasons to make financial decisions: spending, purchasing, investing and hoarding. Spending is food and shopping; purchasing is insurance or cars or house; investing is a pension or stock/shares or ISA; and hoarding is under the mattress or in a jam jar.

Spending is low down the rationality scale, meaning it doesn't last that long and is impulsive. Whereas investing is longer term and well thought out.

So, now we go back to your six things you would purchase:

❖ Where do they sit within this money actions graph? Have you spent all your money on short-term impulse purchases low down the rationality? Or have you invested it all?

I don't think anyone who has done this exercise has answered that they invested it all.

Life is about balance, the time we spend with our loved ones versus the time we spend at work. If we spend too much time on one thing, then other side suffers. It is the same with money, we need to balance our spending and saving, to have a balanced financial life.

## How have you balanced your wish list?

The more money we have the more decisions we have to make. I have already alluded to the millionaires who go bankrupt due to a failure to monitor their spending. What they really should have done was increase their financial IQ to achieve a more balanced approach to their money.

## Assess – What are your personal values?

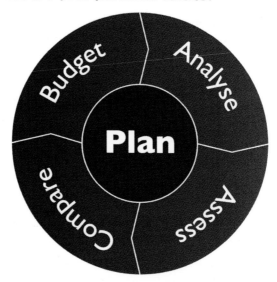

We have analysed what you believe about money, talking about your childhood and asking on what you would spend your money if you won the Lottery. Now we are going to look at your personal values.

## Exercise 2

I'd like you to write on a piece of paper two lists, on one side of the paper 'What do I have?' and the other side 'What don't I have?' These questions relate to financial matters, of course.

| What DO I have? | What DON'T I have? |
|---|---|
|  |  |

We spend a lot of our time thinking about what we don't have, thinking of what we want to buy next and what our neighbour has. Basically, comparing ourselves to others. We spend less time appreciating what we do have. I could bring in here the Law of Attraction but this is not the place. However, I would highly recommend Googling this subject. A book, Are You Worth It? by Liz Almond, discusses valuing yourself and creating abundance is well worth reading. It covers in depth about money mind set and how to improve how you feel emotionally around money to change your circumstances. Liz says 'If you have issues around money management and find it hard to deal with your finances or are in debt, it is probably because you have some self-worth issues which you need to address. Your mind will be accessing past events where you felt bad about maths or in managing money.  For example, if you really hated maths at school, it is likely that you have developed a maths phobia and are suffering from dyscalculia.  This means that every time you attempt something mathematical in the here and now, your mind will revisit the negative emotion from the past event where you linked maths to the negative emotion of anxiety, guilt, embarrassment or humiliation. (E.g. you were made to feel stupid by your maths teacher or you stole money from a friend which you feel bad about.)  You will revisit that bad feeling, so you eventually learn to avoid doing anything financial or numbers related to avoid the bad feeling. The good news is that you can reprogram your mind by using techniques such as Neuro Linguistic Programming, Meditation, Emotional Freedom Technique, Hypnosis and Reiki so that your mind lives in the present not the past. When you are happier about managing figures, you will find it even easier to apply the excellent knowledge in this book.'  For some free money mind set resources such as a journal, money mind set hypnosis and meditations, visit www.insightfulminds.co.uk and to gain advice about how to change your thinking about managing your money.

## Exercise 3

The next exercise is enlightening: What are your personal values? When it comes to any personal value, they will fit into one of these ten categories:

❖ Creativity/personal expression.  This could be in any form, such as acting, painting, speaking or dancing

❖ Professional development.  This could be paying for a course, reading, paying for a mentor or going back to school

❖ Growth of self.  This could be travelling or starting a new job or working for a charity

❖ Family.  This could be spending more time with them or providing for them

❖ Relationships.  This could be going out with friends, treating a boyfriend or husband, or this could be spending time with your partner

- ❖ Health.  This could be a gym membership or a personal trainer or having regular check-ups or paying for supplements

- ❖ Independence.  This could mean a passive income (not an hourly rate income) or having your own space to live without having to rely on someone else

- ❖ Personal legacy.  This could be your long-term legacy for the world or your family

- ❖ Sense of control.  Here, control means you having full awareness and able to make decisions without worries

- ❖ Security.  This could mean more than having a roof over your head, but feeling safe at home and your future being safe and secure

These words should have your own meaning and resonate with you on your own level.

Now you need to decide what are your top five personal values? Don't think long about this, the five should be the first things that come into your mind. Then order them one to five with number one being the most important to you.

**Compare – Where are you now to your personal values?**

Moving on to the next step, we are now going to compare these values.

Let's look back at Exercise 2, the list of 'What I do have', these become your main assets.

## Exercise 4

Compare this list to your top five personal values. Do any match up to your existing spending and which are not in place? How can we be happy in life if we are spending all of our time creating things for ourselves that do not match our personal values? We can't. Time and money need to be spent on what is important to us.

I find a lot of clients have a nice car and a roof over their head, however when looking at their personal values, more often than not they don't compare to what they do have in life. I see this with single women around their 30s. Lots of nice things to talk about having, such as cars and shoes, but when looking at their values, independence is important to them. Their spending or focus isn't anywhere near becoming independent, usually not knowing where to start.

Often money is the pillar of people's happiness, not because money is important but because they are spending money in areas that aren't actually important to them. For example, if they think about learning a new skill and taking piano lessons, they think "I can't afford it" when in fact they can afford it. They simply have the wrong focus and they don't realise it.

For new habits to be created, we must value money, have the right environment and a clear goal.

**Budget –**
"Where are you investing now?" Where is that against your personal value?

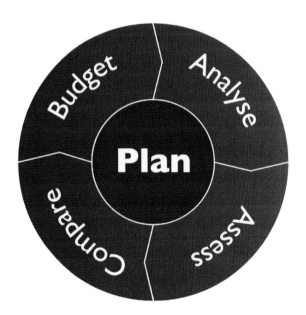

Knowing where you are spending right now is a key element in mastering your money. How will you know what habits to change? How will you know what cut backs to make? How will you see where you are not focusing enough attention?

## Exercise 5

This exercise, if done correctly, can add so much value to your finances, not just currently but in the long term. It is like a business audit, no one wants to do it but once it is done you are pleased to know what needs to change and how well, in reality, you are doing. Some clients are doing a lot better than they believe they are.

The best way to start is to print off three months bank statements for yourself and your partner's income, if you wish to do this as a household. It can be a positive exercise for you to do together, though I have been to clients' houses when, once the partner is out the room, I've been told about loans and credit cards that the other didn't know about. This is not a good place to be with your money.

Once you have printed off the bank statements, run through the transactions putting each one into a section.

1. Fixed expenditures. These are outgoings that you know are going out and how much they are each month, for example mortgage or council tax

2. Set expenditures. You know where the money is spent but you don't know the amounts, for example on petrol or eating out. By making a note of outgoings for past three months, you can average this out to a monthly total.

3. Essential and non-essential items. These are the items that take a little more work, they are often small things and lots of them. Again, they need to be added up, they might even end up with a place on your budget planner all on their own, such as Costa Coffee, if you go there enough. Again, you can average this out into a monthly spend.

Some people like to write it all down. If this is you, use a bound note book as you will want to look back on this. Using your PC is easier as you can save the document – and by using the Excel program, this will add up the totals for you.

There is a budget planner available to download for free on our website, www.evolutionforwomen.co.uk/freebies/

It will provide totals, deduct the income and work out the surplus. There is also a free budgeting video to help you know where things are and where to place items.

| | A | B | C | D | E | F | G | H |
|---|---|---|---|---|---|---|---|---|
| 1 | | MONTHLY BUDGET PLANNER | | | | **TOP FIVE VALUES** | | |
| 2 | | | | | | 1 | | |
| 3 | | MR | MRS | Joint | | 2 | | |
| 4 | (1st )Outgoings | | | | | 3 | | |
| 5 | Gas | £0.00 | £0.00 | £0.00 | | 4 | | |
| 6 | Electric | £0.00 | £0.00 | £0.00 | | 5 | | |
| 7 | Water | £0.00 | £0.00 | £0.00 | | | | |
| 8 | land line Telephone | £0.00 | £0.00 | £0.00 | | | | |
| 9 | Internet | £0.00 | £0.00 | £0.00 | | | | |
| 10 | Council Tax | £0.00 | £0.00 | £0.00 | | | | |
| 11 | car Ins | £0.00 | £0.00 | £0.00 | | | | |
| 12 | Petrol | £0.00 | £0.00 | £0.00 | | | | |
| 13 | Mortgage | £0.00 | £0.00 | £0.00 | | | | |
| 14 | Life Insurance | £0.00 | £0.00 | £0.00 | | | | |
| 15 | Endowments | £0.00 | £0.00 | £0.00 | | | | |
| 16 | ASU | £0.00 | £0.00 | £0.00 | | | | |
| 17 | Health Ins | £0.00 | £0.00 | £0.00 | | | | |
| 18 | Buildings Ins | £0.00 | £0.00 | £0.00 | | | | |
| 19 | Contents Ins | £0.00 | £0.00 | £0.00 | | | | |
| 20 | pension | £0.00 | £0.00 | £0.00 | | | | |
| 21 | Loans | £0.00 | £0.00 | £0.00 | | | | |
| 22 | Mobile Phone | £0.00 | £0.00 | £0.00 | | | | |
| 23 | TV Licence | £0.00 | £0.00 | £0.00 | | | | |
| 24 | Sky TV | £0.00 | £0.00 | £0.00 | | | | |
| 25 | Pets food/insurance etc | £0.00 | £0.00 | £0.00 | | | | |
| 26 | Clothes | £0.00 | £0.00 | £0.00 | | | | |
| 27 | Hairdresser | £0.00 | £0.00 | £0.00 | | | | |
| 28 | Travel (bus/train) | £0.00 | £0.00 | £0.00 | | | | |
| 29 | Glasses/Contacts | £0.00 | £0.00 | £0.00 | | | | |
| 30 | Gym | £0.00 | £0.00 | £0.00 | | | | |
| 31 | Eating Out/Pub | £0.00 | £0.00 | £0.00 | | | | |
| 32 | Cigarettes | £0.00 | £0.00 | £0.00 | | | | |
| 33 | Education | £0.00 | £0.00 | £0.00 | | | | |
| 34 | Window Cleaner | £0.00 | £0.00 | £0.00 | | | | |
| 35 | Newspapers | £0.00 | £0.00 | £0.00 | | | | |
| 36 | Maintenance | £0.00 | £0.00 | £0.00 | | | | |
| 37 | Sports events | £0.00 | £0.00 | £0.00 | | | | |
| 38 | Savings | £0.00 | £0.00 | £0.00 | | | | |

Once you know what is going out each month and how much is coming in, you will know how much surplus cash you have. If you don't have any surplus, but your calculations are showing you should have, you need to go back to your bank statements and make sure you haven't missed any items.

Budgets need to be made and planned into our daily lives. This gives us a framework to work around to make sure that we do not spend outside our means and we know exactly what is in the bank at any one time.

Now put your spending items into one of the 10 personal value areas:

- Creativity/personal expression
- Professional development
- Growth of self
- Family
- Relationships
- Health
- Independence
- Personal legacy
- Sense of control
- Security

You then tally up the totals to establish your top five. Compare this to your original list. How many match up? What isn't in place? What is missing?

**Plan – Action only makes changes**

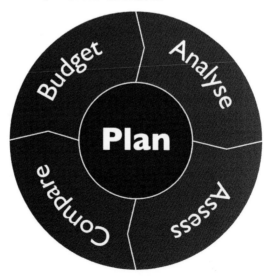

So we now move on to Plan – only action will make changes. It takes six to eight weeks to create new habits.

## Exercise 6

Take a look at your outgoings. What needs to change within your current spending procedure? Where do you need to focus your financial efforts? How can you make those changes?

Something I give a lot of my clients to do is a Financial Detox. This is a great way to get a handle on the changes that need to be implemented. It takes 6 weeks to create a habit . . . so I suggest a three-month programme.

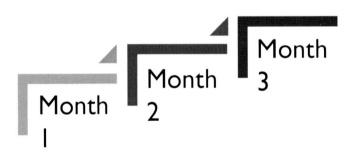

## MONTH 1

Using the budget planner you have completed and using different ways to make cut backs (listed further on) plus seeing what you could instigate reductions on, such as making lunches and only eating out once a month, reset your budget to a DETOX budget. Try to increase the spare capital to 20% of your salary. So if you earn £1,000 a month this would be £200.

The amount will then become your savings. If you haven't saved before, you will need a section on your planner for this. If you have saved, try to increase the gap by 20%.

To ensure you don't over spend, a lot of clients withdraw the amount they are budgeting to spend and place the cash in separate jars. Spending within the 'allowance' for any particular item ensures the overall budgeting is adhered to. Once the jar is empty, you don't put more in.

It is important to tell family and friends what you are planning. This isn't about you being lacking in any way, but about you wanting to improve and take positive steps towards your financial freedom. Knowing what parties are coming up and what meals out you have planned is key. And if you have forgotten to put one in the budget, be prepared to tell the hosts you can't make it. Have the conviction to follow through with your plan. You will be cheating only yourself if you do otherwise.

Another great way to understand your finances better is to have a note pad – in your bag, on the kitchen side or at your desk at work – to compile a list of items that you DIDN'T buy. These are items you would have normally brought. Maybe you even missed them off your bank statements when reviewing your out-goings. This is your spending journal. Make a note next to each item if it was something you WANTED or something you NEEDED. At the end of the month add up the total, see how much you would have spent. If you still NEED those items listed, the decision is yours on whether to go ahead with the purchase.

## MONTH 2

Once you have that first month out the way, you can treat yourself. Give yourself an allowance to have an extra meal out or a day trip for the family. This is, of course, if you have been strict enough in your detox month. You may have found some additional ways to make adjustments to provide you additional savings.

Set your revised budget, use the jars to manage the cash flow if needed and put aside those savings.

## MONTH 3

By now, you will be a professional budgeteer, this isn't about being frugal but knowing where all your money goes. This is the foundation needed to be able to start to plan out the next phase. The quicker you can get here the better.

You now have a money management plan. You have the foundation to build and take things to the next level.

## 52-Week Challenge

One savings exercise that some online followers have enjoyed is the 52-week challenge. You start with £1 on week one and each week start to increase it by £1, the balance of savings being £1,378 at the end of the year. Some struggle with around £200 in a Christmas month (if you started week 1 in January) however it might be Christmas that you are saving for.

If you would like to budget for Christmas, we have just such a budget planner on our website for you to download:

http://evolutionforwomen.co.uk/freebies

| Week | Deposit Amount | Account Balance | Week | Deposit Amount | Account Balance |
|---|---|---|---|---|---|
| 1 | £1 | £1 | 27 | £27 | £378 |
| 2 | £2 | £3 | 28 | £28 | £406 |
| 3 | £3 | £6 | 29 | £29 | £435 |
| 4 | £4 | £10 | 30 | £30 | £465 |
| 5 | £5 | £15 | 31 | £31 | £496 |
| 6 | £6 | £21 | 32 | £32 | £528 |
| 7 | £7 | £28 | 33 | £33 | £561 |
| 8 | £8 | £36 | 34 | £34 | £595 |
| 9 | £9 | £45 | 35 | £35 | £630 |
| 10 | £10 | £55 | 36 | £36 | £666 |
| 11 | £11 | £66 | 37 | £37 | £703 |
| 12 | £12 | £78 | 38 | £38 | £741 |
| 13 | £13 | £91 | 39 | £39 | £780 |
| 14 | £14 | £105 | 40 | £40 | £820 |
| 15 | £15 | £120 | 41 | £41 | £861 |
| 16 | £16 | £136 | 42 | £42 | £903 |
| 17 | £17 | £153 | 43 | £43 | £946 |
| 18 | £18 | £171 | 44 | £44 | £990 |
| 19 | £19 | £190 | 45 | £45 | £1,035 |
| 20 | £20 | £210 | 46 | £46 | £1,081 |
| 21 | £21 | £231 | 47 | £47 | £1,128 |
| 22 | £22 | £253 | 48 | £48 | £1,176 |
| 23 | £23 | £276 | 49 | £49 | £1,225 |
| 24 | £24 | £300 | 50 | £50 | £1,275 |
| 25 | £25 | £325 | 51 | £51 | £1,326 |
| 26 | £26 | £351 | 52 | £52 | £1,378 |

You can download a blank version to complete each week via our website.

**MORE MONEY SAVING IDEAS**
## Saving on energy bills
You can change spending habits if you look at your house and go round room by room. There are little things you can do to save money on your energy bills:

- Turn down your thermostat
- Close the curtains as the sun goes down to stop the heat escaping
- Turn off the lights when you leave a room
- Turn off the TV when no one is watching it
- Don't leave items on charge unnecessarily
- Fill up your washing machine or dishwasher, they use less water and electricity on one full load than two half loads
- Make sure none of your taps drip

You can get a free energy check from the Energy Saving Trust website, which gives you a free report on how you can save money on your bills, http://energysavingtrust.org.uk/insulation/home-energy-check.

## Saving on shopping
- If your journey to work sends you through a shopping centre, change your route to work if you can.
- Tell your friends that you are going out for dinner only once a month instead of once a fortnight.
- Meet your friends in their homes or your home instead of in the coffee shop.
- When you are food shopping, try some of the shop's own brand items, they can be just as good yet half the price.
- If you are thinking about Christmas shopping, look at our blog for handy tips on how to budget for the holiday season. http://evolutionforwomen.co.uk/blog

- If you want to buy new clothes, think about what is already in your wardrobe. Is there anything that you could sell to make some money to buy the new item? Does it go with what you have in your wardrobe? Will you wear it once and then leave it because you haven't got anything to wear it with.

- Cut up your credit cards. Maybe keep one for emergencies, but put it away in a box so it's harder to get to it.

- Apply for a 0% interest rate card and transfer your balance from your current card.

## Saving on investments and insurances

Many people overpay on life insurance policies for years without realising. It's well worth getting a fresh eye to look at your policies and see whether they are relevant for you now and whether they could cost you less.

If you have stocks, shares or ISA's, it's worth examining them to see if they are still as effective as they were when you took them out. ISAs interest rates change all the time and you could be losing out.

## General savvy saving tips

Set aside as much of your salary as you can for saving and investing, even if it's only a few pounds as it will add up over time. A general good rule is to have three months' essential outgoings in a savings account for emergencies.

Build up an emergency fund from one of your guilty pleasures. Look at what you spend out for something that is really unnecessary, such as a takeaway coffee every morning or that takeaway meal during the week because you can't be bothered to cook. It may sound small but that will build up over time and you will be surprised at how much you can save.

If you have some surplus money to put away each month, use it first to start paying off the highest interest debt you have. Getting rid of a debt quickly is better for you in the long term and then you can invest more as you don't have that monthly payment to contend with.

## So, where do I begin?

The best way to start is to set a goal for yourself, something that you really would like for you and your family, such as a holiday abroad or a new car, something that really gives you a push to get moving.

Write it down, preferably where you all can see it every day – such as stuck to the fridge. This is a good way of reminding yourself why you are changing your habits.

Work out how much you are going to save. Even if it's a small amount, everything helps.

Find a money box or tin to put change into and leave it in an accessible place where you can easily put the coins but not be able to take them out so easily.  Or set up a standing order straight from your bank account into a simple savings account, so you won't miss the money.

The state-owned National Savings and Investments bank (NS&I) states that people who set a savings goal save faster and up to £550 a year more than those who don't.  So, get saving and change the habits of a lifetime.

## Top tips for getting your finances under control and work your way out of debt

Here are a few ways of getting our finances back into the black.

## Look at your finances

Take your head out of the sand and have a good look at your finances. Assemble all your paperwork.  Find out exactly how much you owe and to whom.  As a rule, if your debt repayments take up more than 20% of your total income, you really need to take steps to cut back.

## Make a budget

Once you know how much you owe, you can then set a monthly budget schedule for repaying those debts.  Don't try to do it all at once because that could put you into a deeper mess.  Work out a realistic monthly payment that you can afford.  Talk to you creditors to see if you can agree a schedule of payments. Many welcome this step as they realise that you are serious about repaying the money.

## Think before you spend

Do not borrow any more money or take on any more loans or credit cards until you have paid back your existing debts.

### Use cash

Each week take out a set amount of cash, which is within your budget and covers your basic needs, such as food, petrol and other essential bills. Put your card where you can't get at it.

### Bills

Revisit all your outgoings and see what you could save money on. You could switch your utility bills to save money and pay by direct debit as most of them give you discount for doing so. Revise your home and car insurances and switch annually to save money. Your TV, broadband and phone should be evaluated to check if you can save money by switching or splitting providers.

### Credit cards / Loans

Switch your credit card or loan to providers with more favourable interest rates. One way to get rid of your card altogether is to switch to a Balance Transfer card, which will give you a 0% interest rate for a set time period. While you are in that time period, try your best to pay off the whole card. If you can't within the allocated period, look to moving again.

### Store cards

Who has them anymore anyway? They charge the highest rates by far for any credit, they are the worst way to build up debt, so get rid of them now. Cut them up and start to pay them off. It's worth remembering that some bank accounts offer cash back in certain stores, so you can earn yourself money by shopping.

### Bank accounts

Examine your current account and see what you are getting from it.

Also look at the interest rates you are paying on your overdraft or any payments you are making for added extras that you may not be using. There are numerous online bank accounts as well as the ones we know well, so shop around.

## Savings
If you have any savings, check the interest you are receiving. You could probably find better rates by switching to a new provider.

## Mortgage
The biggest expense you have each month is most likely to be your mortgage, so it is important that you get the best possible deal. It is always worth, in the first instance, going to your current mortgage lender to see what they can do for you, or going to see a financial adviser, who can scour the market to work out if it's worthwhile to switch.

## Protection insurances
Its worthwhile examining your insurances, such as your mortgage protection, critical illness cover and income protection . . . as you could save money here. It may be that what you took out several years ago is no longer applicable to you, or you may be under-covered. A review will make sure you have adequate cover but you could also save some money if you have a savvy financial adviser who can hunt out the best product for you.

# ONLINE Money Makeover Programme ™

*"Don't wait until you are ready to take action. Instead, take action to be ready".*

~Jensen Siaw

Are you ready to take action and make a difference with your finances? There are often two types of action takers. Those who can attack the challenge full on and embrace the mind set and changes in their life. Baby steps in taking action to get small but consistent results or even big changes which create whole shift with their money. The second kind of action taker is those who want to and intend to but are unsure where to start and need that little more structure to take them through the process. For those clients, or for those who just want to ensure they haven't missed any thing, I've created an online version of the Money Makeover Programme.

This consists of a weekly video breaking down each section for you to take step by step positive actions. If you think you will put this book down and have every intention to take action but know you won't, sign up for the online version which will make you accountable and give you actions to do in a more manageable way. Those baby steps will after a few weeks start to create RESULTS!

We will also have bonus material which can be viewed within the same programme for you! For example if you are in business we have a bonus edition for you.

The Money Makeover Programme TM is available online, if you need additional support or talking through this process. Go to www.evolutionforwomen.co.uk/moneymanagement

# CHAPTER 8
## Using psychology to straighten up your personal finances

There is a widely known theory in psychology that helps to explain how people behave, this is known as Maslow's Hierarchy of Needs, devised by American psychologist Abraham Maslow in 1943. He believed that people are motivated to achieve certain needs and when one is fulfilled they will move up to the next one. If the basic needs are not met, people are motivated to meet them. The longer they are not met, the more an individual is motivated . . . for example, the longer you go without food, the hungrier you become and want to eat.

There are five layers or stages in this theory, defining the various layers of need from the basic up to spiritual enlightenment. The five stages are shown in this diagram:

Maslow explained that you cannot or will not move up each stage until you have satisfied your needs in the lower stages. It is a pyramid shape due to the levels of importance of each stage.

It makes sense. If you don't get enough sleep, you can't function properly at work. If you don't get enough food or water, your health will suffer.

Maslow believes that everyone is capable of moving right up the hierarchy to the top, which is self-actualisation. However, the progress up the stages can be disrupted by incidents in life that prevent people from meeting lower level needs. For example, the loss of a job or the death of a spouse.

It's a simple way of setting out priorities in life.

## So how does this reflect our finances?

Not all of these can be attributed directly to money, however it is easy to see the link. For example, we usually worry about being able to pay the mortgage before we think about having to pay for the phone bill, our pension or put money into our savings accounts.

If we want to get our priorities straight in life so that we can move up the hierarchy, it makes sense that we need to get our financial priorities right.

Let's draw the triangle again and put in some different descriptions that link to finance:

At the bottom, we have **Survival Money.** Simply put, we need to bring into the household enough money so that we can pay the necessary bills. This does not include any of the niceties, such as TV, phone or broadband, just the basics. Take a minute to work out the cost of your survival.

If you are falling short at this level, you need to take steps to change it. If your income isn't meeting your needs, you may need to reassess your needs. What are the shortfalls? Do you need to look for another job, or move house or look at benefits you may be missing out on. It is crucial at this stage that you can look after yourself.

The next level up is **Safety Money**. It is at this level that we look at being able to pay for the next level of needs, which make us feel safe and secure in our lives. We start to look at the family unit and ensure that we are protecting them as well as ourselves. This is where we look at insurances such as life insurance, income protection, pensions and critical illness cover. Financial risk exists at every stage and it is here where you don't want to outlive your money.

It is at this stage where we start to have savings and put away money for life's unexpected turns . . . from simply a broken boiler to the more complex one of redundancy or serious illness. The general rule here is between three and six months of savings.

If you fall short at this level, there are ways of making the most of your money. How much do you have each month once you have paid all your bills? Find out this figure and work out how to distribute it in the most logical and beneficial way for you and your family.

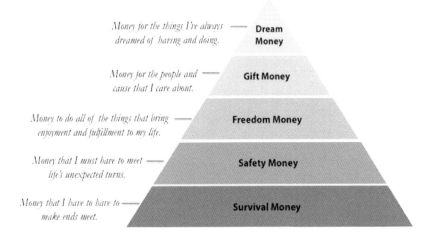

You may need some help with this as insurances can be tricky to calculate. Talk to a financial adviser who can help you establish what you can achieve.

Next we have **Freedom Money**. Here, we are at the level where we can start to do the things that we enjoy, the type of things that we really want to do rather than have to do, such as travelling, re-training, further education, holidays, new houses or cars and hobbies. This is where we attain a desired standard of living rather than one where we feel stuck in. Maslow's level here is love and belonging. If you attribute this to finances, this is where you gain enjoyment and pleasure in life.

We are now quite high up the hierarchy and if you are here, you have achieved a great deal.

However, according to Maslow's theory, you still need more. The next level is what we call **Gift Money**. This is where you wish to attain financial independence so that you can plan for a comfortable retirement with the same levels of lifestyle that you are having while you are still working. If you are here, you have some spare cash to give away to good causes. It is also about giving money to your family in order to help them out. So as you have moved up through Maslow's hierarchy, you have already secured your survival, your safety and your financial freedom, it is now time to give to others who are less fortunate than yourselves.

Finally, we attain the highest level, which is **Dream Money**. It is the hardest to reach and the most elusive. Maslow believes that only one in ten of us will ever attain this level. Here, you are able to buy the things that you always have dreamed about, that amazing home or the supercar. It is also where you are in a position to give your money away as you desire, for example sponsoring your local football team, because you can and want to. You may also wish to contribute money to your family to make sure that they are living comfortably. Financially, you will be in a position to be able to work out your estate to secure your children's futures.

If you want to get to this point, how will you achieve that? Firstly, you need to decide what it is you want. What do you want to be? What would you like to do? What do you want to own? It may be that a change of career will fulfil you or you may need to become involved with activities that align themselves to your values and purpose in life.

By breaking down your financial goals into manageable chunks, you can more easily work out what you need, want and desire. You are then able to create a plan that will take you to financial freedom. Starting from the simplest of goals, which could be to cover your outgoings, and then building on attaining that extra income that will allow you to save and create more wealth.

So, what to do you do next?

# CHAPTER 9
## The Money Matrix ™

Once you have established the foundation of your money, you know what you want for your own personal perspective, you will know what you spend your money on each month, you will know how much you have spare and how much you can afford to save.

So the rest is easy, right? This is where it gets more interesting.

As we have discussed in previous chapters, putting value on why you created these new habits is one of the main key elements to success. Doing it for the sake of it is not enough. We are driven by two things . . . either avoiding pain or gaining pleasure.

With the Money Makeover Programme exercise, we looked at 10 key personal values:

- Creativity/personal expression
- Professional development
- Growth of self
- Family
- Relationships
- Health
- Independence
- Personal legacy
- Sense of control
- Security

You may have a list of goals that you want to achieve now, perhaps paying for a specialist evening class, building a deposit for your first home, going back to college or joining a gym.

## STEP 1: Goals and Vision

A way I like to chart these goals isn't literally writing a list but creating a vision of these elements of my life. They aren't necessarily objects but a feeling or a way of life. You can do this by collecting magazines or having access to a colour printer. You start to compile images of those goals and you can either pin them on a board or stick them to pieces of paper. Some people do this with pic images via apps. The important point is that you spend time to find the right images. What you focus on is what you achieve, and that they are something you can see regularly.

## STEP 2: Cash Flow Allocation

Practically speaking, you then need to break down those elements, with a realistic savings plan. Ideally not all your monthly income will be spent on 'fixed or set expenditures'. If you totalled up all of yours, what percentage is it of your monthly salary? If you put your 'essential/ non-essential expenditures' in play money, how much of a percentage is it of your monthly salary? For example:

£2,500 per month total

| £1,250 | 50% Necessities |
| £250 | 10% Financial freedom |
| £250 | 10% Long term savings |
| £250 | 10% Education |
| £250 | 10% Play |
| £250 | 10% Give/charity |
| **Total** | **£2,500** |

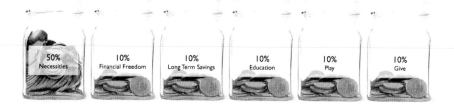

| 50% Necessities | 10% Financial Freedom | 10% Long Term Savings | 10% Education | 10% Play | 10% Give |

## STEP 3: What are you worth?

Take a moment to work out what you are worth right now until your retirement age, without increasing your salary.    Take your annual salary or, if you wish, the household annual salary, multiply this by:

❖ Your retirement age – let's use 66 years old (though it might be older) minus your current age. For example:

> £20,000 per year
>
> 30 years old take away 66 = 36 years
>
> 36 x 20 = £720,000.00

You are your own cash machine.  That is a lot of money, and when we work it out like that, it really show us how much we all must waste. How you spend your time making and spending money matters.

## Step 4: Pot allocation

These simple images represent how most people spend their money.

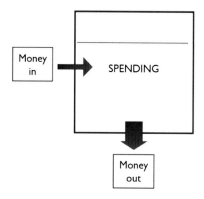

The box represents your main bank account, with money coming in each month. The arrow pointing down is your money going out each month with your spending. Above the line is spare money. However, this is often spent also, some might be put into savings for emergency. Little is invested.

We have grown up in an age of spending, buying what we want when we want it, not *need* but *want*. The process continues by taking out more finance to fund this spending need. We don't save for a car, we get a loan and inadvertently invest nothing for our future.

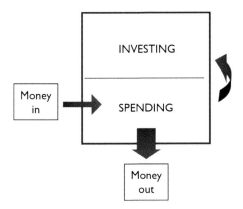

The smart way of managing finances is to create an income from income. Use your initial income and put efforts into investing or saving. Creating an income to spend will produce longer term benefits. Passive income is very much what many people will be looking for in the future.

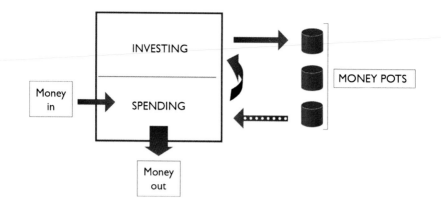

The purple spotted arrow represents revenue return or income money coming in. As this increases, providing you with more money to play with, you can achieve your personal value goals and create more income to be invested. This is how those with money seem to have it easy. In fact, they have had to get educated and smart with money.

I've already mentioned that it is important to have an emergency pot of at least three times income. This is to ensure you do not have to use credit (loans and credit cards) to purchase items, therefore creating debts. Even if the credit card is at 0%, at some point this will run out . . . and when you want to transfer it to another offer, you could be charged a transfer fee. This is also a monthly commitment, even if it's a minimum payment, it is an amount that you are spending that cannot be invested.

Loans have their initial interest and fees added right from the start, before you even make a payment. Then, the total debt is repaid over a period of months or years. Again this is a monthly commitment and you are paying back interest as well as the debt itself. If you can save and pay for the item outright, this is better in the long term.

A mortgage is quite possibly the biggest debt that any individual may have in their lifetime. Here is an example of how much you are paying back even with a small loan of £97,500 over 25 years and a low interest rate of 2.74% for two years:

- With a two- year fixed interest rate of 2.74% that will revert to Standard Variable Rate, 4.50% in 2016, for the remaining term of the mortgage, the total amount to be reimbursed is £204,939.00

This means that you will pay back £2.10 for every £1 borrowed. Can you imagine if I lent you £100 but I asked for £210 back? When you put it like that, it makes you think. Your mortgage is not just £100 or if you are lucky it won't be £100,000 either. The quicker we pay back debts the more this allows us to free up capital to invest and not be paying interest on it. The example below shows a repayment mortgage over 25 years with the client making over payments, thus reducing the debt, paying off the mortgage quicker, 10 years quicker.

Your mortgage debt over time

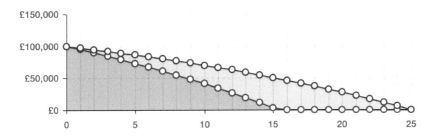

This illustrates how a £200,000 mortgage spread over 25 years, with overpayments of £500 a month, will save £82,772 in interest and reduce the term to just over 15 years.

# Mortgage repayment calculator

**Enter your details, and experiment with overpayments**

Currency ⦿ £ ◯ $ ◯ €

| | | |
|---|---|---|
| Amount borrowed | £ 200,000.00 | |
| Number of years | 25 | |
| Interest rate of mortgage | 5.5 | % |
| Overpayments made per month | £ 500.00 | (optional) |

Calculate

**Here's what you'll pay**

| | | |
|---|---|---|
| Monthly payment | £ 1,728.17 | |
| Total paid | £ 285,680.45 | |
| How much is interest? | £ 85,680.45 | |
| Time to pay off | 13 years, 10 months | |
| Amount saved by overpayment | £ 82,772.04 | |

You can find our recent blogs and guides regarding mortgages, from first-time buyers to those wanting to re-mortgage and offset mortgages, here:

http://evolutionforwomen.co.uk/services/whole-of-market-mortgage-broker/

You can see the importance of clearing debt. I should say the highest rate of interest debts are an important part of your financial journey. Once you are out of the red and into the black, you can seriously consider where to save and how to invest.

## Back to pot collection (step 4)

So you're ready to start saving? Before you start to become a massive long-term investor, the starting point is to create some basic savings accounts in which to place the emergency funds and the personal 'goal' money. If that is a regular amount or just a fund to access, the easiest way to manage this is to ring-fence the money to ensure that it cannot be accessed daily. You must be sure the monies are not included in your monthly outgoings for bills. Some banks will allow you to have several accounts and even 'name' them. Alternatively, you can keep a spread sheet for your reference.

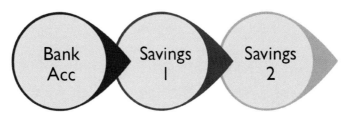

Things to consider:

What is 'Inflation?'
Inflation is the rate at which the general level of prices for goods and services is rising and, consequently, the purchasing power of currency is falling. Central banks attempt to limit inflation, and avoid deflation, in order to keep the economy running smoothly.

Therefore, if all your savings are sitting in a standard bank account or savings account with an interest rate lower than the rate of inflation, your money is losing value. The rate of interest should be higher at the very least than the rate of inflation. This is an issue to those relying on savings to provide an income when interest rates are low.

Compound Interest
As mathematical genius Albert Einstein once said:

> *"Compound interest is the eighth wonder of the world. He*
> *who understands it, earns it. He who doesn't, pays it."*

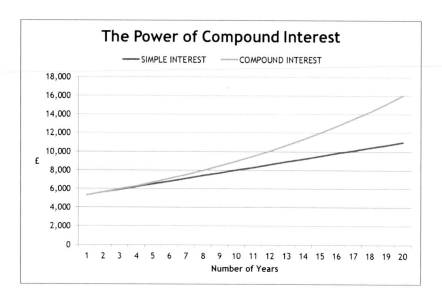

The Power of Compound Interest

SIMPLE INTEREST    COMPOUND INTEREST

This is where the interest you earn on your savings is added to the initial investment pot . . . and you then earn interest on the interest. As the graph shows, this increases your overall investment or monies earned. In this example, we highlight how an investment of approximately £5,800 would provide the client with a return of approximately £11,000, a £5,200 profit – almost doubled the money over 20 years. With compound interest – that is interest on the interest – the return would be £16,000, an additional £5,000.

## Step 5: Financial Priorities

Now it is time to look at your financial priorities, the hierarchy for any financial plan starts with living for today - putting food on the table. As a financial planner we have to ensure that clients are not putting themselves or their family's basic living needs at risk. Unless a client has substantial wealth (as in millions), protection or insurance to pay for your basic living for today is next on the priorities. That is income to pay for those things, a pension for future retirement, savings and then investments.

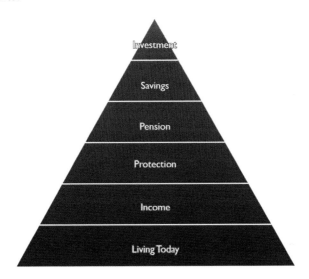

## 1. Living today

Women make 85% of the purchasing decisions and have significantly more control over the household finances than they had 10 years ago, a survey claimed.

Three-quarters of women said they thought they now had more control over the payment of domestic bills than a decade ago, according to the research by car giant Vauxhall. And 56% of men agreed with this.

At the same time, 61% of women in a relationship thought they had more say over savings accounts, while 51% of men thought their partner was now more involved in this aspect of their finances. But while the majority of women felt they now took overall control of the domestic finances, the majority of men still thought that they were in charge.

And while 54% of men claimed they took care of domestic bills, only 9% of women thought their partner took the lead in this area.

For this reason, the day-to-day purchasing power of women has increased and we have become great at finding the best deals to provide the family with living essentials. This is our basic human need. Of course, everyone has a different version of what is 'essential'.

Source: https://www.theguardian.com/women-in-leadership/2016/feb/03/how-advertising-industry-fails-women
http://www.manchestereveningnews.co.uk/business/property/women-hold-pursestrings-1023819

## 2. Income
Income to provide for our families is at Stage 2 as this pays to put food on the table. Some have that level of drive and determination to provide more, women tend to spend this additional money on everything apart from themselves.

The difference in the average salary between men and women, according to a Government report, is 19.1%. For every £1 that men earn, women earn 80p. This is based on both full and part-time work.

The Office for National Statistics stated in its November 2014 survey that the gap is actually 9.4% based on full-time hours excluding overtime.

It says that in regards to part-time work, this is reversed and it is actually women who earn more, 5%. However, this can be explained by the fact that women tend to work part time throughout their working life whereas men may work part time only at the beginning or end of their careers.

## Why do women earn less?

There are several reasons why women tend to earn less than men. For example:

- There are more women in lower paid jobs, such as healthcare where it is found that average wages are £40 less a week than the national average. This is where 80% of the workforce are women. There are fewer women managers, and when they do get to management, they are paid less than their male counterparts. Women dominate the workforce in childcare, 94%, and in secretarial positions, 92%, however, only 7% are engineers and 20% are architects, which are much higher paid positions.

Additionally, when weekly pay rates were researched, the gap was even bigger because men tend to work longer hours than women, they are more likely to do overtime and they receive bigger bonuses.

The gap varies in different industries. The Office for National Statistics found that in the transportation, mining, storage and quarrying sectors, women earn on average around 3% more than men. In finance, insurance, technical, scientific and utilities, men earn significantly more than women, on average around 27%.

## 3. Protection

There are several different types of protection requirements. I find with clients their perceived risk is actually not correct.

Life and critical illness insurance is a lump sum or monthly sum paid out by the insurance provider. This can be taken out for a particular sum assured and over a particular term required. Life insurance covers the person insured in the event of death while critical illness insurance covers the person insured on diagnosis of a defined critical illness.

### Why would you have life and crucial illness insurance?

You would have this kind of insurance to cover a mortgage or debt, to ensure a continuation of the lifestyle that your family has come accustomed to, or provide income to care for young children until they are of adult age.

**How do you know what level of critical illness you are getting?**
There is a guide call Defacto, which has been put together by an independent researcher of financial products. This produces star ratings based on a selection of factors.

Each insurance company covers a certain amount of defined medical definitions, ranging from 25 to 166. Some of these definitions are what is referred to as ABI – Association of Business Insurers – meaning out of those particular amount of definitions some of them are up to the ABI standard.

We don't like to think that anything bad will happen to ourselves or our families, however according to the ABI study in September 2014, around a million people each year are forced to take time off work due to a serious illness or an injury.

Think about it. If you had to be absent from work because you had a serious illness or you had an injury which meant you couldn't do your job, how would you or your family cope with the loss of income? Your employer may have protection that will enable them to pay you sickness pay. However, this could be a fraction of your salary.

According to reports from Personnel Today, just 12% of employers support their staff for more than one year if they are off sick. The Government's website says the minimum Statutory Sick Pay an employer has to provide after three continuous sick days is only £88.45 a week for a maximum of 28 weeks.

How would you pay the monthly bills? Some people rely on government benefits, but will they be enough to cover your bills?

One way of approaching this is to take out Income Protection insurance. This is a long-term insurance policy that will help you if you have a serious illness or injury. This starts after your sickness pay has stopped from your employer.

It is different to Critical Illness insurance, which pays out a lump sum if you have a specific illness. The Government's website states that most common causes for income protection claims are for illnesses that would not be covered under Critical Illness policies.

**Income Protection**
Long term. You can get cover for one-year, two-years or until you retire. It replaces part of your income if you cannot work at all. It is based on a percentage of your salary, the usual amounts are 50% or 70% and payments are tax free.

It will pay out until you start working again or until the end of the policy, or you retire or the worst case scenario that you pass away.

You have to wait a period of time before the payments start, called your deferred period, which is agreed when you take out the policy. It is usual that these payments do not start until your sick pay stops or other insurances stop paying. The longer you have chosen the waiting time to be, the smaller your monthly policy payments will be. The normal time can be 4, 8, 13, 26 or 52 weeks.

It will cover most illnesses that leave you unable to work (you need to check the policies as they all differ). You can claim more than once from one policy while it is still valid.

It is worth checking with your employer before you apply for this insurance just in case their sick pay would be more than enough for you to live on.

Think about the long term. Would your employer's sick pay cover your income for 12 months or more? If not, it is worth getting advice as to the best protection you can get for you and your family.

## 4. Pension
Consider this: in 1900, the average life expectancy for a woman was just 50 years of age. Today, it is 81 years of age. Thanks to advances in living conditions, diet and medical care, we are all living longer – but

few of us stop to think what impact this will have on our later lives.

According to a study by Public Health England published in April 2016, women aged under 65 are likely to spend almost a third of their lives in retirement, such is their future life expectancy.

This might sound like a blissful way to kick back and relax for a few decades, but it means most women will have to commit much more to their pension than they realise – or spend many years having to cut their cloth extremely tight.

The amount you receive will depend on a number of factors – when you start paying in, the pension product you choose, your salary, and the size of employer contributions to your fund, to name a few examples.

There is a basic state pension available to those of retirement age, but it is minimal.  The current maximum allowance available through a state pension is £119.30 per week.  Most people choose to 'top it up' by contributing to a private pension scheme.

Even auto enrolment workplace schemes might not be sufficient to give you adequate retirement funds, with the required contributions in 2016 set very low.

The Office for National Statistics (ONS) has revealed that just under 50% of people do not have a private pension. This means that when they retire, they will be relying on the State or any investments they have to fund their income.

Pension companies are struggling to fund individuals' retirements mainly due to an ageing population and low interest rates. Many schemes are in debt and others are generally under-performing. So is it worth getting a private pension, or should we look to save our money another way?

**Why bother?**
About 12% of people surveyed by the ONS said that they wish they had

never taken out a pension because it is under-performing and it won't provide enough income in their retirement.

Reuters revealed that many pension schemes are in deficit, which means that they don't have enough funds to pay out what they will finally owe to their pension holders when they retire.

Pensions money is invested in the stock market, so depending on how good your fund manager is, your fund could even decrease if they make poor judgment in their investment choices or their charges are high, or if the stock market struggles. These are risks that we all take in order to give us a good pot of money when we retire.

You have the control, you can transfer your pension into a better performing one, you can change your broker and you have the power to decide what stocks and shares your money will go into.

You also cannot get to your money until retirement, so you have to wait before you can spend the money. This can be a good thing for some people who would be tempted to spend it before they retire and, therefore, leave themselves with nothing.

### What type of pension to have?
**Private pensions** mean that you have to fund them yourself, but it is a secure form of paying for your retirement and you have total control over who you choose as a fund manager and where your money is held.

**Employer pensions** have the possibility of your employer contributing towards it, too, with some even matching what you are putting in, which is an added bonus. However, you do not have control over which company manages your funds.

All pensions are tax efficient, too. If your payments come straight from your gross salary, you won't pay tax on them. If they don't, you can claim the tax back.

A pension also provides security. It's a guaranteed income for the rest of your life once you retire.

Remember, it is worth starting early. Many young people going into their first job will not even think about pension contributions, but with longer living and the State not being able to provide, it is worth taking the step of starting your pension early to build up a decent fund. Who knows what will happen in 30 years' time, we may not even have a National Health Service to rely on.

A pension is still a very good way to save for your retirement and should be thought about as part of your saving strategy. It is worth getting good solid advice before making a decision. A financial adviser can help you choose what is right for you.

## 5. Savings
### Saving versus investing: what's best?
When you are financially stable and ready to start planning for the future, you might want to consider long-term investing – for example, in a stocks and shares ISA alongside a standard savings account.

This can grow your nest egg more quickly than standard savings, but bear in mind that the value of investments can go down as well as up and you may not get back the amount you invested.

Depending on how bold you want to be, there are a number of risk profile options available, which a financial adviser can talk you through. A medium-risk investment might not have the same high returns as high risk, but it offers greater stability.

Being young, you also have the benefit of choosing a longer 'time horizon' for your investment. However, your investment plan should be mapped to your personal objectives – for example, if you're hoping to buy a house in two years, choose that as your 'time horizon', so you can cash in the money for a deposit when the right moment comes around.

Scottish Widows research offers that human beings are focused on the immediate, by our nature, wanting satisfaction and fulfilment right now, having little interest in putting them off. In the world of finance, that means we want to see the guaranteed benefits of our money immediately instead of wondering about our future, which is intangible and delayed even if we know that it means our lives in the future will be secure.

## As a nation, how do we plan for the long term future of our finances?

This is the question that the Scottish Widows report was looking to answer. We do know that we must save for the future, but so many people ignore it or put it off. Their report is based on an online survey of 5,000 plus adults in the United Kingdom and was conducted in March 2014 by the independent research agency, YouGov. It asks about the attitudes to saving and how people can manage their money more efficiently.

Caroline Rookes, CEO of the Money Advice Service, says: "This report suggests that many people instinctively understand the need to cut back when the going gets tough. That's good news. It's not quite such a positive finding that while people refuse to countenance reducing their phone or mobile usage, they find it comparatively easy to cut back on protecting their assets and their families against an unwelcome turn of events."

Around 19% of people in the UK have no savings at all. It doesn't sound like a big number until you put it into number of people, so that's around 12.4 million, one quarter of the adult population.

There are 17.5 million people between the ages of 35 and 49 years old. Yet a massive 55% think that individuals should take more responsibility for saving more.

The average amount in savings per person during 2013 was £2,882.

When put under pressure, people will cut back on eating out, entertainment and more than half would stay in more often.

About 33% of us are saving proportionately more than we were two years ago but more than half are actually saving less

More men (50%) than women (46%) said a preference for spending their money was a barrier to saving.

The report notes that many people are still not sure what long term means and how much we need to save to cover emergencies, holidays and our retirement. Everyone wants to retire early but they still want to spend money now rather than thinking about putting it away for the future.

Read the full report here: http://reference.scottishwidows.co.uk/docs/2014_sandi_report.pdf

## 6. Investments

Investments are a great way of making your money work well for you. In the economic climate where interest rates are very low, you could be losing out by keeping your money in a savings account in the bank. Investing in stocks and shares could help you achieve greater returns and assist you in reaching the long term financial goals you have been thinking about for your retirement or your children's futures.

It is a big step to take for the first time when you think about investments and investing for your future. There are many different options to consider. It can be overwhelming and downright confusing for anyone who has not looked at it before.

Here is a quick guide to what you need to think about before you start and how investments work.

### Are you ready to invest?

You should have several things in place before venturing into the world of investments. There is an element of risk involved with any investment, some more than others, so it is worth thinking about how you feel about taking a risk with your cash.

You don't need to be afraid of it, just aware that you need to be prepared for the fact that you could lose some or all of your money depending on the risk you are taking. You need to consider:

### Understanding the risks
If you have a strong long-term plan and plenty of spare cash to fall back on, the risk element is not so much of a concern, but if you think that you will have sleepless nights if the market is not performing as you would like it to, it's worth going for something with reduced risk.

### What do you want to achieve?
Set a clear goal for yourself. Do you just want a regular income or are you looking for a lump sum in the future? This will tell you how much you need to invest and in what time-frame. This will also tell you how much of a risk you should be prepared to take.

If it is a short-term goal (less than five years), you may want to stick to savings as your investment may not return what you need in a short period if they fall in value. If it is a medium-to-long-term goal (five to 10 years-plus), investing is more appropriate. However, you need to think about your age and state of health to make sure that if a long-term investment falls in value, you still have the means to earn to build it back up again.

### Regular income versus lump sum
If you are comfortable with risk and know what you want to invest in, a lump sum is the way to go. If you are more cautious and want to see a regular return, regular savings is the way forward.

A lump sum is investing all your money at one time
This is where you would invest, say, £10,000 on the stock market at once, whether it is in bonds, shares or units in a trust. They are bought at the same price and you can benefit from any price rises straightaway. The downside is that if whatever you have invested in goes down, your money will too. This is where long-term investing can work as it gives

the market time to recover.  So you have to keep a regular eye on the markets.

<u>Regular savings, known as 'pound cost averaging'.</u>
This is where you regularly invest a set amount each month into your chosen shares over a period of time.  If the share price goes down one month, you will be able to buy more shares for your money, so by the end of the time period you could end up with more shares than if you had put in a lump sum.  Also, if the share price drops, only the money you have in at that time will be affected rather than the whole lump sum.  The downside is if the share price continues to rise over time, you will not benefit as much as you won't have all of your money invested.

## Do you have savings?
## Prepare for the unforeseen
Make sure that your income is protected before you invest.  It's worth ensuring that if you couldn't work for an extended period of time that you and your family will be able to pay the bills.

## Getting your priorities straight
Make a start by matching your income sources against your income needs and then work out which sources will pay for which needs.

If you don't have enough to cover your survival step, there are serious changes that need to be made in order for you to be able to pay your bills.

If you find you only have enough money to pay for survival and safety at this point, you will at least have the comfort of knowing those two critical bases are covered.  It is important at this stage that you look at what insurances you have put in place for you and your family and ensure that they are adequate for your needs.

## Thinking about the future – what else to consider?
Begin to view your income not as just a way to pay the bills but as a means to funding a life — the life *you* want.

Many people do not think about a Will, saying that they won't need it for a long time yet, or that they don't have much and it will go straight to their nearest family member anyway. That is not the case and you must ensure that somewhere in writing is what your wishes are exactly in the event of you passing on.

Making a Will ensures that everything is sorted out quickly and efficiently and without argument amongst family at a most emotional and stressful time. Dying without making a Will (intestate) means that a court relies on a set procedure set up by the State to distribute any assets and it does not consider any wishes of the deceased.

A Will also helps to reduce Inheritance Tax liability in the sense that, if it is looked at early enough, measures can be put into place to move monies and assets in order to reduce the amount that lies above the tax threshold, which in 2016 was £325,000.

Setting up Trusts within a Will can be extremely valuable in Estate Planning for a number of different reasons.

When it comes to protecting assets and controlling the distribution of your estate, Trusts are essential and advisers can provide a variety of different solutions depending upon your objectives.

Despite changes in legislation there are still some valuable reasons for establishing Trusts in your Will and there are still inheritance tax benefits. Having certain assets "ring fenced" in a Trust can ensure that your children are not paid outright.

Should a surviving partner become infirm and need to go into long-term care, funds in a Trust would not feature in terms of local authority means testing. This is subject to certain criteria.

Often, the solution to a complex situation can be with the use of a Trust, which can be created as a stand-alone document that is set up whilst still alive and comes into force immediately, or if written into your Will, upon your death.

Some of the more common Trusts found in modern Wills are used for protecting your property after your death. You may wish to leave your property to your children but by using a Trust this will allow you to provide for your spouse or partner for the rest of their life.

Avoiding Inheritance Tax legally can be an accounting or legal minefield but the one guaranteed route, wholly endorsed by the Inland Revenue, is by way of a Discretionary Will Trust, either set up in your lifetime or within your Will to be effected on the first death of a couple.

### 10 Reasons to make a Will

- You would have control on what happens to your estate.

- To avoid disagreements on how your assets are divided. Sadly, it is increasingly common for relatives to take court action amongst themselves, splitting families apart.

- To avoid your family becoming involved in unnecessary costs or delays, which could amount to tens of thousands of pounds.

- You choose who looks after any young children.

- If you were cohabiting without being married, the lack of a Will could mean your partner would have no automatic right to any of your property and could be evicted.

- To ensure there is sufficient money left to comfortably provide for your partner or spouse.

- To prevent your family home being sold to distribute your estate. You can make this position clear and ensure your spouse is not left homeless.

- To avoid your estate paying tax unnecessarily – leaving less to distribute amongst the family.

- To provide protection for your business partners, ensuring there is no forced sale of your business.

- To provide you with peace of mind.

**Power of Attorney**

This defines who is responsible for any individual if they become incapable of dealing with their own finances or day-to-day needs, physically or mentally. It provides for the carer to talk to doctors and solicitors with the vulnerable individual knowing that they are being looked after properly and their needs are being dealt with correctly. The mistaken belief is that Power of Attorney is protection for our elders should they get Alzheimer's disease. However, an accident or illness can happen to anyone at any age.

It's never too early to put a Power of Attorney agreement in place . . . and those who have elderly relatives should talk about this situation while they are capable of discussion it lucidly. If you don't have such an agreement in place, making arrangement can be protracted and heavy costs can be incurred. This can be very unhelpful if you are trying to organise a care home for an elderly relative and you cannot get to their finances to pay for it. I know a friend who took months to get this sorted out for her grandmother who was in hospital in the meantime as she had no one at home. The hospital kept wanting to get her out because they needed the bed, but there was no money to pay anyone to look after her anywhere else.

**TAX**

This is a massive area of consideration when making financial decisions. Income tax, inheritance tax and capital gains tax must be taken into account. There are several factors to take into consideration.

- Your assets may be gaining value but they are also increasing your income tax position.

- Keeping assets in certain places can cause inheritance tax issues.

- Cashing in the wrong investments with capital gains tax to pay.

These are just a few of the areas that clients' needs to consider in financial planning. This is where an experienced financial planner would be able to work through the implications of all the different areas and make recommendations on the impact this will have on the client.

## Where do I go from here?

You need to insure yourself and your money to protect the ones you love. It costs less than you think and you need to safeguard some of your income for your retirement and whatever life throws at you to ensure that your children will be safe no matter what happens to you.

Don't just accept what you see on the high street, there are better rates and better choices, take investment seriously and look into it thoroughly. Talk to a financial adviser to help you make the best decision for you and your family. You don't have to take risks, there are safer options, and you will feel far more in control once you know exactly what everything means and why you are buying into it.

I believe it's not that women need extra help. They need different help. They need different products and levels of protection compared to men. They want to be able to understand exactly where they are putting their money as it affects their whole family. And because women think about all things and all people at once compared to men who compartmentalise, they need to know a lot more about what they are paying for.

A great place to start is the Evolution for Women financial check-list below – answer the questions Yes or No. If there is a 'No', it might be something you wish to consider and get some advice on.

## FINANCIAL CHECK LIST

### 1 EMERGENCY FUNDS POSITION

| | | |
|---|---|---|
| Do you have three times the level of regular monthly financial commiments? | yes | no |

### 2 PENSION POSITION

| | | |
|---|---|---|
| Do you have suffient income in retirement? | yes | no |

### 3 ESTATE PLANNING

| | | |
|---|---|---|
| Do you understand your inhertiance tax position? | yes | no |
| Do you have a Will in place? | yes | no |
| if yes and you have children - did you set up guardianship for your children within it? | yes | no |
| Do you know if your estate would benefit from a trust? | yes | no |

### 4 MORTGAGE POSITION

| | | |
|---|---|---|
| Is your mortgage guaranteed to be repaid before retirement? | yes | no |
| Have you had full independent advice on this mortgage? | yes | no |

### 5 PERSONAL and FAMILY PROTECTION POSITION

| | | |
|---|---|---|
| Does your life cover, full cover the correct mortgage and any debts outstanding? | yes | no |
| Does your life cover, full cover the correct mortgage term and any debts outstanding term? | yes | no |
| Does your life cover extend to cover over and above the mortgage for all other life style costs? | yes | no |

### 6 CRITICAL ILLNESS COVER POSITION

| | | |
|---|---|---|
| Does your cover, full cover the correct mortgage and any debts outstanding? | yes | no |
| Does your cover, full cover the correct mortgage term and any debts outstanding term? | yes | no |
| Does your policy cover you for the amount of illnesses you would expect? | yes | no |
| Does your cover extend to cover over and above the mortgage for all other life style costs? | yes | no |

### 7 INCOME PROTECTION POSITION

| | | |
|---|---|---|
| Does your income protection position cover at least 50% of your income for long term illness? | yes | no |

*no advice is given with this check list - all clients personal circumstances are different *

www.evolutionforwomen.co.uk

## Hands on approach

We've discussed so much so far and you might be thinking, "How can centralise all this information?" "How can I keep on top of my growth and know how I am doing with my money?"

If you are wanting to take your finances up a gear and really get ahead of your money, would you like to have a tool that will allow you to manage your overall personal finances? I am happy to share with you a personal finance software tool that is loaded with all the features you need: online banking and bill payment, account management, budgeting and investment tracking.

Do you use online banking? You can download your banking transactions, upload them to the software. You can then allocate income and outgoings towards set categories, thus allowing you know what you are spending your money on each month. The software learns how to automatically categorise and clean up downloaded transactions. From this you can allocate several accounts including savings.

You can follow your investments and bring your portfolio into focus with support for stocks, bonds, mutual funds, and more. View the find out more go to total value of your investment accounts or the performance of individual stocks and mutual funds over time. It can provide an overview of your finances. Do you know your net value? The information shown includes account balances, upcoming and overdue transactions and reminders, and exchange rate information. Clicking on an account or choosing an account from the drop-down account list will take you to the register for that account, where you can enter transactions or reconcile the account against a statement.

Clicking on a transaction reminder will display a window where you can automatically record the transaction. It is a fantastic tool that will allow you to manage everything I have covered.

*"Decide what you want your life to look like and then decide what vehicle is going to get you there"*

To download a copy and find out more go to
www.evolutionforwomen.co.uk/moneymanagement

(Availability subject to provider support and user experience)

# CHAPTER 10:
## The economy and how it affects investment decisions

There is a saying that if China sneezes the United States of America catches a cold. During 2015 and 2016 China played a massive part in how the stock market globally performed. Below we discuss how this became the case, what volatility it created and if there are alternatives to investing in the stock market.

In August 2015, China decided to change the way they calculated their exchange rates, causing depreciation in the Yuen and estimated losses of US$5trillion dollars. It is believed that China did this to make exports more competitive and therefore increase their overall economy as there inflation rates are low and they are seeing a decline in spending, including fuel consumption. Together with this, the slowdown in Asia's market would give the US a chill.

China's stock market until June 2015 was picking up pace due to new laws allowing funds to invest and firms to offer shares to the public, along with changes in mortgage lending, it was inflating the stock market. This took a down turn when there were concerns over the unsustainable growth, companies started to freeze their share options and causing investors to sell their stock, according to Bloomberg indexes China's Year to date return is 14.5%.

Due to the slow economic global growth, oil prices have dropped. It's a simple supply and demand issue. Oil is one of global products which countries like China need to import and countries like US are over producing it to export it. Although China would benefit from this drop in price, their consumers aren't demanding it, thus causing a drop in revenue to those who are exporting, so they mass produce even more to make up their margins.

For the first time in seven years, the US increased their interest rates by 0.25%, as they felt their economy could withstand the change. There is much talk of this happening in 2016 for the UK also, however the Bank of England need to be sure it will not reduce inflation and spending due to increasing mortgage payments and loan rates. This change in the US market did cause the stock market to decrease with the demand and price.

These three key areas have caused the stock market to be volatile, meaning confidence has fluctuated and therefore so have the prices.

How do all key areas affect the stock market?  Let's take this back a step and discuss what areas could affect the stock market and why.  So far we have mentioned interest rates, inflation or deflation, imports or exports and foreign markets.

Do you remember your last work do, when everyone was talking about it and how much they were looking forward to it and caused a buzz in the office? Or do you remember when there was a meeting coming up and everyone was a little worried of what the outcome might be... The stock market is fuelled by these highs and lows. These 'Chinese whispers' of what might be the longer term outcome of certain facts which are changing by the minute.

If a company launches a new product which is cutting edge, this would cause a buzz and people would want to buy those stocks – meaning the prices increase with demand. If companies are not doing so well, so start to sell off their stock, then so might other investors, causing stocks to drop in price.

Inflation is the rate at which the price of goods and services increases. It is the result of several factors, including a rise in the cost of manufacturing, transporting and selling goods. When inflation is at a low rate, the stock market responds with a surge in selling. High inflation causes investors to think that companies may hold back on spending; this causes an across the board decrease in revenue and the higher cost of goods coupled with the drop in revenue causes the stock market to drop. Deflation is when the cost of goods drops. While deflation sounds like it should be welcomed by investors, it actually causes a drop in the stock market because investors perceive deflation as the result of a weak economy.

When the economies in foreign countries are down, companies cannot sell as many goods overseas as they used to. This causes a drop in revenue, and that can show up as a drop in the stock market. Foreign stock exchanges also have an effect on the stock market. If foreign exchanges start to fail or experience sharp drops, then that kind of activity can cause investors to anticipate a ripple effect, resulting in a drop in the stock exchange.

Therefore when China changed the way they calculated their exchange rates to improve the cost of exports this caused a drop on the stock market also. When China changed their laws around how funds could be invested and lending issued to borrowers it initially caused people to invest more in the stock market however this was a fake increase and people quickly realised that it was a temporary boom. Investors and companies quickly jumped out of the markets, freezing their shares and selling them off also. Causing prices to further drop...

Higher interest rates mean that money becomes more expensive to borrow. To compensate for the higher interest costs, companies may have to cut back spending or lay off workers. Higher interest rates also mean that company cannot borrow as much as it used to, and this has an adverse effect on company earnings. All of this adds up to a drop in the stock market. Thus linking back to inflation, the more people spend, the more a business has in revenue and the more their stock prices increase.

So where does the oil prices fit into all of this? China, Europe and Japan have slowed their need for oil (fuel) as less people are using cars and companies aren't transporting as many goods. The demand has dropped, thus the price of oil has dropped to attempt to sell more of it. This is one of the first signs that the economy has slowed, supplying a third of the world's energy resources. Oil is produced by several key country's however one the biggest consumers is China. America started to produce massive levels of oil in recent years due to having a high demand and political reasons with foreign relationships. Oil slumps don't have a direct effect on the stock market but are a key indicator on what is happen in the global economy.

So you see the global economy is linked. These changes in the economy change the stock market prices causing peaks and troughs in the stocks prices. This is described as volatility. The measurement of volatility is called 'standard deviation', they are bench marked or averaged by 'expected return'. If a share price fluctuates between 4-5 per cent this would be classed to have low validity. If the investment fluctuates greatly between from the expected return and has a higher standard deviation this would be classed as being 'volatile' and higher risk. Timing and assessing what 'might' happen is crucial when buying and selling shares. This is known as a 'spread', the difference between the buying price and selling price. Funds managers would be looking for a share which has standard deviation with a low volatility providing a good expected return without the risk.

Typically if you invest in one company's shares this would be classed as high risk, as you are putting all your monies into one company. Diversification is where you spread this risk into not just different funds like the stock market – equities but also other forms of investment which aren't reliant on the global economy volatility which we have discussed so far, these are cash, fixed-interest securities and property, thus making a balanced portfolio

Diversification is measured by correlation between assets classes. Correlation is the relationship between two different types of assets, taking into account performance. This is measured with number from +1 to -1 the extent to which assets classes tend to rise and fall together. Fund managers or investors would be looking at the correlation to see if they are cancelling each other out or one is outperforming the other. Another way of diversification in a portfolio is to invest in different industries or difference counties, UK, Europe and worldwide.

*"Diversification is protection against ignorance. It makes little sense if you know what you are doing."*
Warren Buffett

## An Efficient Frontier
### The Power of Diversification

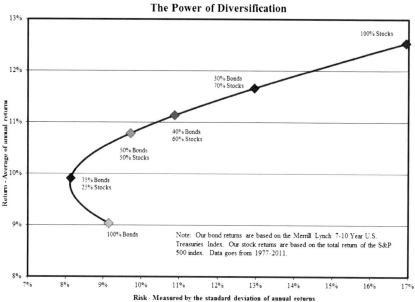

www.youngresearch.com

Respected American economist Harry Markowitz devised his own 'modern portfolio theory' which is a mathematical framework for putting together a portfolio of assets so that the expected return is maximised for a given level of risk. This is defined as variance. His theory puts forward the concept that an asset's risk and return should not be assessed by itself but by how it contributes to a portfolio's overall risk and return.

This graph above highlights diversification using the theory. This illustrates the highest returns are 100% stocks, however, it also has the highest risk, whereas 50% stocks and 50% bonds reduces the return by just over 1.5% and the risk reduces by a near 8%.

This theory considers the expected values, standard deviations and correlations of assets in the portfolio in order to calculate the portfolios expected return and volatility of a portfolio.

So if not just equities, where else could you look to invest? We briefly mentioned cash, fixed-interest securities and property. Let take a closer look at those.

- Cash is also known as deposit based investments – these are where the capital doesn't grow but the capital receives an interest return either monthly or annually. These would start with your typical bank and building society accounts with online only accounts or full banking facilities with cheque book to including deposit accounts, which usually operate with a notice period for withdrawing funds – though this is usually a variable interest rate and is in line with the Bank of England. Fixed interest products usually tie monies into an account for one to five years, providing a slightly higher return but there is limited access to the money without having to pay penalties.

- National Savings products are also 'cash' or deposit based investments, with a wide range of types of products available.

- Premium bonds offer a money prize tax free, and the more you buy the more you could win. Funds can be withdrawn without penalty at any time.

- Income bonds provide a monthly income and can be open from the age of seven or can be purchased for those less than seven years old. The bonds can be cashed in at any time without notice or penalty. These are not always available as they are issued in tranches.

- Guaranteed equity bonds provide 100% return of capital at maturity together with potential growth linked to the performance of the FTSE 100 over the term of the bond. Any gains would be subject to capital gains tax.

These kinds of savings are classed as low risk as the capital will be returned to the investor. The Financial Services Compensation Scheme provides compensation to deposits, although limitations are in place, £85,000 per investor or £170,000 for a joint account.

- Fixed-interest investments, as the title would give away, provide a fixed interest rate and income, often referred to as bonds.

  - Amongst these are gilts, known to be a safer way to invest as the State is unlikely to default on payments. Gilts are available to a wide range of investors so it can be competitive. They can be bought and sold for amounts above or below their face value providing a coupon. They can be short or longer term up to 15 years. Another benefit is they are being traded on the stock market sometimes 2% to 3% above market rates. Gilts come in two forms: fixed interest and index linked. With the interest rate fixed, a long-term investment does run the risk of not keeping up with inflation, whereas this would not happen with an index linked product.

- Corporate bonds are not issued by the treasury but by companies themselves as a way of raising funds. Therefore, they are more risky as the company could default on payments, but they can provide a higher return due to the increased risk. They pay a fixed rate of interest and have a redemption value at the end of the bond period.

## Investing in property

According to the Nationwide House Price Index, published by the Nationwide Building Society, the average price of a house in the UK increased from £59,587 to £189,002 in the 25 years to December 2014.

We have seen slumps in the market in recent years (2008, however by 2010, the market was level again and by 2014 we were seeing increases in property values.

Property in the UK is seen to be a stable investment and to some preferred as it is something physical to possess rather than a piece of paper. Putting residential homes aside, property investing isn't as simple as writing a cheque to a fund manager for them to invest for you, unless of course you use a property finder or agent. There are many layers to consider before jumping into a property purchase.

There is often a larger lump sum regarded for a deposit and there could be costs involved to prepare the property for letting, as well as solicitors and mortgage fees. However, investors still see the potential of large returns even over a five-year period so they feel property is a limited risk with high returns. Typically, an investor would be looking to not only receive a growth return but also an income return. This is determined by the rental yield.

'Rental yield' is the total amount of rent minus the running costs (mortgage payments, insurance, repairs and maintenance etc.), divided by the total amount invested to purchase the property (that should include all fees, including tax and legal fees).

One way of investing in property without directly buying a property is by investing in listed property companies on the Stock Exchange, however this could be classed as high risk as you are investing in one particular industry. Via unit trusts or open-ended investment companies that are pooled investments, the investors are buying a share in a portfolio of properties. Often smaller investments can be made and the risk is spread across a range of properties.

To have a diverse portfolio, it is wise to consider ISAs, which are a tax free range of savings vehicles, consisting of a cash ISA, which is comparable to a deposit savings account, and a stocks and shares ISA, which was limited to £15,240 per in the tax year 2015/16.

The ranges of stocks and shares that can be held are:

1. Shares
2. Unit trusts and OEICS – equity, bond, cash and money-market based
3. Investment trusts
4. Gilts
5. Corporate bonds etc., many of the products we discussed so far.

The obvious benefit of investing via an ISA and using your allowance each year is the tax benefit. Any interest received is paid gross and is not taxable. Capital gains tax does not apply when disposing of the assets although losses cannot be offset against it either.

All the other options are subject to tax or CGT in some shape or form. Property rental income is subject to income tax and is run like a business where some costs can be deducted, such as maintenance of the property. Allowances for mortgage interest was due to be phased out from April 2016. Gains made on the sale of the property would be subject to CGT but annual allowances apply - £11,000 each or £22,000 jointly is the personal allowances, gains over this would be payable at 1% or 28% for higher or additional rate tax payers.

Apart from open-ended investment companies and gilts, most other investing options are subject to CGT, open ended investment companies are exempt, meaning the funds can grow free of any future tax. However, income tax is payable at 20%, which can be claimed back by a non-taxpayer, higher rate and additional rate taxpayers would pay 25% and 32.5% respectively.

Dividend income, the first £5,000 of dividend income in each tax year will be tax-free. Sums above that will be taxed at 7.5% for basic-rate taxpayers, 32.5% for higher-rate taxpayers and 38.1% for additional-rate taxpayers. These tax levels took effect on April 6, 2016. No tax will be deducted at source; taxpayers must use self-assessment to pay any tax due.

Pensions, of course, should not be forgotten as they have a lifetime allowance far more than any other investment (£1,250,000 in 2015/2016) providing an annual allowance of £40,000 (2015/2016), along with a weekly allowance of income tax free.

Taking all these factors into consideration, the next element to be considered, is you? As an investor, what are you looking to achieve? What are your feelings towards the different levels of risk? And what kind of returns where you hoping for? Are you more interested in receiving an income now or in the future or were you hoping to achieve capital growth longer term? Did you want to access any monies quickly and by how much? If you were to pop it away, how long would you be comfortable investing the money for?

Therefore, by assessing your current portfolio position, how diverse is it? How much is in easy access emergency accounts, providing you low returns? Or how much is in volatile funds giving returns but they keep you awake at night?

Going back to the efficient frontier theory, by assessing your portfolio ask yourself, where are you on this chart. Are you 50% bonds and 50% stocks and shares? Are you at different ends of the scale? There is no right or wrong answer in terms of what this 'should' look like, but it should represent your needs as an investor.

For example, if you are very cautious and prepared to take only a small element of risk but you are investing in single investments within a limited industry, then this would meet your investment needs.

Other considerations are age and, therefore, where you are in your life cycle. If you are middle, possibly you would be looking to save and invest and can afford to invest medium to long term, whereas someone closer to retirement is likely to want to protect their capital to ensure there is enough to pay an income into retirement.

Lastly the investor's personal tax position must be taken into account and maximised where ever possible.

# CHAPTER 11
## Financial milestones/life events

The Personal Financial Life Cycle. What is this about? What do you need to know?  And how does each stage of your life affect your personal finance choices.

### What is the Personal Financial Life Cycle?
Traditionally, financial planning and tax planning have been carried out ad hoc throughout individuals' lives.  We tend not to think about our financial strategy until something comes up where we need to scrutinise our spending.  This usually occurs when applying for a mortgage or making a Will.  It seems that we purchase these products without any regard for what else we might need to complement them or how our lives will change in the future that could make them useless to us in one, five or 10 years down the road.

Most people follow a similar pattern with their personal finances. People should continuously refine and tweak their financial plans to meet their changing financial desires and needs.  This becomes the life cycle.

### Why do we need to think about it?
Each stage of our lives is influenced by many factors, including personal values, life choices, major life events and the needs of each physical stage of life.  Some factors are expected, such as getting married or buying a house, and some are unexpected, such as redundancy or illness.

There are also a host of life conditions that are all relevant at different stages, including age, marital status, income, education, health, dependents and the economy. Some plans follow throughout our lives, such as savings or a mortgage, others are more critical at specific stages, such as making a Will once you have children.

Creating and following a life cycle plan gives you a better understanding of the rise of financial risk over time and what you will need to think about at set periods in your life. It can help you create a plan where you can manage all your finances together, allowing you to possibly finish paying off your mortgage early because you deliberately set up a savings plan to do it or you bought investments that gave you the ability to pay for your children's education or their first property.

## How to manage your wealth over time:

Within this life cycle, there are three basic stages of wealth – protection, accumulation and distribution. These are explained as follows:

### 1. Wealth Protection – 18 years to 45 years

This is where you should be building financial security for your life ahead, doing cash management by setting goals about your career, lifestyle and family commitments. This is where you need to do credit and debt management to avoid getting into too much debt, protecting yourself against economic downturns and insuring yourself in case you were suddenly to have an accident, for example.

### 2. Wealth Accumulation – 35 years to 64 years

This is where you have reached your peak in earning terms and are building your nest egg for your children's future and your retirement. You need to think about your children's futures and your retirement plans.

### 3. Wealth Distribution – 65-plus years

This is where you are spending your savings and pension during retirement and also planning what you are going to give to your loved ones when you pass away. These three stages give you an overview of how your money grows and falls throughout your life and helps you see where you may need to tighten up on your spending.

## What are the stages of the financial life cycle?

So, now we come to the Financial Life Cycle. This is split into six stages, each one with its own set of challenges and decisions.

**The first stage is the Childhood stage from age 11 years to 18 years**
All finances are the responsibility of your parents or carers at least up until 16 years old and you do not have to worry about where the next penny is coming in from until you start making choices about your career and what type of lifestyle you want for the future. This is where parents can help their kids, by teaching them the realistic value of money and what children need to do in order to achieve the goals that they have set themselves.

Parents can help their children by taking them into the bank or building society and opening a savings account with them. They can show them that having a job, such as a paper round or doing chores at home, can earn them money that they can put into this account and grow the fund so it can pay for a large item they are longing for.

Children can also have a book that they can enter all their receipts, and they can keep a record of jobs/chores done and money earned in it. This can help reinforce good financial record keeping for the future, especially if they have to do their own tax returns eventually.

Talking about money and how much things cost can help children with their career path decisions. It is important to have open and honest discussions with children about money as it will give them the knowledge about what they need to save for in the future and what will drain their income, such as property and children. This is especially important if they have an ideal style of life they want to keep. They may need to go to university, so saving for those fees will become crucial, or if they are learning while working, saving for a car may be more important.

So, get their learning and experience started as early as you can and build on it as your child gets older. Reward charts are a good place to start for younger children, earning money from doing chores will help the whole family.

### The second stage is the Young Adult stage from 18 years to 24 years

There are a lot of factors influencing your finances right now. This is a time of rapid personal growth as you become independent from your parents and start your journey through life.

If you are at university, the challenges will be how to make the most of the little money you have and if you have a student loan, you need to maximise the use of that loan, so that you don't have to borrow more. The Money Advice Service can tell you how much you will need to pay for university fees and how much the average living expenses can be: www.moneyadviceservice.org.uk/en/articles/student-finance, and Money Saving Expert gives some great tips to help you make the most of this money: www.moneysavingexpert.com/students/student-guide

If you have decided to go straight into a job, you can start to save. This is the time to think about what you want from your career and where your aspirations lie. On-the-job training is a bonus as you don't have to pay for it, however if you want a specific career and your job is not in that field, you may have to finance your training yourself.

You may need to buy a car, so saving for that is vital. Or maybe you would like to get your feet on the property ladder, then you will need to curtail your spending as saving for a mortgage can be a momentous task.

You have to spend to accumulate. This works in different ways. In order to build a good credit rating, you need to take out some credit, such as a credit card or bank loan and prove that you can use it and pay it back within the schedule. The first thing you can do to help your credit rating is make sure you are on the electoral register even if you live with your parents or are at university . . . and you can do this as soon as you turn 18. The Money Advice Service is again a good place to start to find out what you need to do: www.moneyadviceservice.org.uk/en/articles/getting-credit-for-the-first-time

If you wish to buy a car or purchase a house, you will need to think about all the insurances and other payments that go along with them, so you need to make sure that you have money in the bank throughout the month to pay these premiums.

It is worth getting some good solid financial advice at this stage. It will help you plan your financial future well and will also open your eyes as to what you will need to think about as you get older, such as starting a pension now will give you a much bigger retirement pot than if you were to wait until you are in your 30s. Now is the time to save, save, save.

### Starting Out – Meet Amy

Amy is a first time buyer, she has been renting previously but returned home for a year to save a deposit to buy her first house. She has saved £10,000 and her parents have given her another £15,000 towards the purchase.

Amy works full time as a marketing manager, she loves her job but doesn't enjoy the commute into London. She would love to buy in London however the house prices are just too high and outside her buying power.

Amy had considered buying with her boyfriend but she is concerned about her deposit and the money her parents have given her being passed on to her boyfriend if they separated or if Amy was to pass away.

if Amy was to pass away.

Amy has learnt from the newspapers and television in the past seven years that as a first-time buyer she needed to have little or no debt in place to buy her first home, that having credit cards and loans was not a good idea. Therefore, she has a low credit score from her credit file due to having only a £500 bank overdraft.

Thoughts to consider:
Amy could look at buying with her boyfriend and protect her £25,000 legally by writing a Will or by instructing the conveyancing solicitor to put in place trust paperwork that will ensure the money is returned to Amy should she split up from her boyfriend, forcing the house to be sold. This may allow her to buy closer into London in a location she is happier living. Also, it may reduce the travel costs into London.

Subject to credit score lending, Amy could consider building up her credit file. This can be done in several ways but can take time, which in an upward market means she could end up paying more for the same house in six months' times. One way to build her credit file would be to speak to her bank about a credit card and use it once a month for a small purchase but then clear if off each month. Ensuring she is placed on the Electoral Roll at her parents' address is also very important.

---

Predicting your own future is impossible. One thing that is certain is that you will face lots of change.

The lives and careers of women starting out today are very different to those faced by their parents. You will face risks of persistent unemployment, climate change and continuous technological innovation.

You will be healthier and live for longer than your parents. Between education and retirement, you could have a 50-year career.

**Your career won't be static**
It's likely to involve different working patterns, different employers, different sectors, maybe even different countries. You may need to learn new skills along the way, and you may be surprised by the course down which your career takes you.

You may want to marry and start a family; but that doesn't mean you have to compromise on being financially, socially, spiritually independent.

**So here's my advice**
Don't enter this phase of your life without knowing your options. Develop skills, learn to strive for financial independence.

According to figures published last year by the National Insolvency Service, while the number of bankruptcies overall is down in England and Wales, young women are now more likely to fall into personal insolvency or bankruptcy than men. The gender gap is particularly noticeable when it comes to young adults, with 22.2 of every 10,000 women aged between 25 and 34 applying for bankruptcy or another insolvency status, compared with 21.2 of men the same age. This is the first time that the number of women applying for debt relief has overtaken men.

---

**The third stage is the adult with or without children from 25 years to 34 years**
If you have been to university, this is the start of your working life, if you have been working already, you will be in the throes of building your skill base to improve your career. It is in the early days, however, when you need to be aware of the financial risks that you may be taking, such as getting a mortgage, having children and keeping your health.

On the plus side, you have a fairly long period of working years ahead, so your ability to earn is seen as low risk. However, there are also large expenses looming ahead of you, such as mortgage and children. And these come with a higher risk. What is the risk? Well, what if something happens to you that could stop you from working; therefore stop you from bringing any money into the household? How would you afford the mortgage payments and feed the children? These are factors that have to be taken into consideration when you look at mortgage payment protection, critical illness protection or income protection. All these insurances will help you, but they also incur a cost, which you need to plan into your monthly budget.

It is worth establishing a fund of about between three to six months' worth of your monthly salary as an emergency fund so that you have something to fall back on. It is normally at this stage that the need for credit is at its highest and managing this well will stand you in good stead as you get older. If you can save, it is also worth creating a fund for any children you have, whether it is for their education or for when they want to buy their first house or get married. Long-term investment now will give them a bigger nest egg when they turn 18 or 21.

The age of new mothers is rising, however this is still the most common age to have children in the UK and so there are several things that you need to consider in advance of their arrival, such as reduced income while you are on parental leave, purchasing all the things that come with a baby and also life insurance should the worst happen once you are a parent.

Once you have children, you should think about writing a Will, not just so that they will be financially secure if both parents should die, but who will look after your children if they lose both parents. You don't want to leave it to the State to sort that out. It's worth making sure they will be looked after by the people you trust, so a well written Will is essential.

**Working women – Meet Zara**

Zara has been married to Richard for four years, they brought their first place together 10 years ago and moved to a larger house six years ago. The move and the wedding cost a lot of money and has meant that they are paying for a mortgage and paying for credit cards that they haven't managed to clear.

They feel they are paying too much out each month and are unable to save. They feel they don't have a handle on their finances and want to start getting ahead.

They have equity in their current home and they wonder if it would be worth clearing the credit cards with a mortgage instead.

<u>Thoughts to consider:</u>
The first thing to do is for them both to list what credit cards they have. Listing the company, the interest paying rate (not what it would be if they made a purchase), when the rate runs out and what it reverts to, what they are paying each month and if it is the minimum payment or not, what is the minimum payment % (usually 3% to 5% of the balance), what is the credit limit and it is also finding out what offers the company might offer as a balance transfer rate, and if there is a transfer fee.

Once Zara and Richard know this information, they will be able to see which credit cards are on a zero rate or a higher rate. The aim should be to have as much of the credit cards on zero per cent without paying any or much of a transfer fee. They may need to make a calendar note of when offers are available from and make a note of when any rates finish. Once they know how much total debt needs clearing, I would usually suggest they divide the total by either 12, 24, 36 or 48 months, giving them a monthly amount to pay back and a time to clear all the debt within. The monthly amount needs to be affordable, however, as it is an over payment.  And if one month they need to reduce it  they can do.

It isn't often advisable to take this debt over a longer period, like a mortgage.  By doing this, you are paying more interest.

I would then like to see what other spending Richard and Zara are in the habit of doing, see if they are able to either clear the debts sooner or start saving towards back-up/emergency funds.  We would usually like to see clients not have debts in place and making long term saving plans.  However, it would depend on individual circumstances.

---

If you have a successful career and you are finally making the money you deserve; do you think about how you're going to make that money last?

It's time to think about turning surplus cash into savings that can start working for you.  Not just in the immediate term but for your future, too.  One day you'll want to step away from your business or job for good – invested savings will make that a reality.

**So here's my advice.** Don't be passive in this.  Every phase of your life can be controlled by you when you create options for yourself.  You can develop the skills, mentality and financial independence.  I'll help you to get them and keep them.

You shouldn't be afraid or intimidated to invest your savings.  At Evolution for Women, we make sure investing isn't scary and help you to plan for life after work without using impenetrable jargon.

But the truth is that in order to build the wealth you want for your retirement, travel plans or Trusts for your children, you need to invest.  But once you start investing, you will find it is not as hard as you think.

---

**Starting a family – Meet Claire**

Claire is a mum of three, with two of her children at school and one at nursery. She struggles to keep up with all the family commitments and the pressure of being a mother. Her partner is dad to one of the children and he works long hours. Claire manages all the household and financial bills per month but wonders what else she could do to support the family. She has been looking for part-time jobs to build up her own financial pot because when she separated from her first partner she was left without many career options due to looking after the children.

<u>Thoughts to consider:</u>

Without taking benefits into account as this would affect what she can claim, if she is already, Claire may want to consider some basic savings plans, such as an ISA, to put away as much of her own salary as possible. She is unlikely to have a pension or long-term savings in place so starting to get into the habit of saving a little would be important. Often mothers find more ways to spend any additional income on the children. Claire needs to consider her longer term financial requirements.

Families have a long list of financial needs they should consider, from writing their Wills to ensuring that, should anything happen to the child's respective parent or care giver, a plan is in place financially to look after that child. Life cover is the most obvious, however, there are several ways this can be put in place. They should also consider a Trust for this policy.

With the joy of starting a family, having your first child marks the start of the most significant financial change of your life. That will last for the next 20 years.

A recent study by the Centre for Economics and Business Research found a typical parent can expect to spend £231,843 raising a child born in 2016. That's an increase of 65% since 2003. Imagine how that will change over the next 12 years.

The average UK parent will spend more than a third of their take-home pay just to be able to afford one child, with the costs highest between the ages of one and four years old.

In a child's first year, parents will spend £11,498, rising to £63,224, between one and four.

Being a mum today will be very different to the experiences of our mothers and grandmothers. Being healthier and living for longer than your parent's means your finances will have to support you and your family for longer.

**So here's my advice.** Don't enter this phase of your life without any options. Have the skills, have the mentality, and have the financial independence. I will help you have them and keep them.

Saving for your future should start today, just as your finances will be stretched like never before. You will also want to protect your home if you are unable to pay your mortgage, and all the other important financial expenditures in life.

I know these may be the last things you want to think about when you are about to take a positive step in your life, but now can be the best time to consider your financial plan, for you and your new family.

## Entrepreneurs – Meet Charmayne

Charmayne started her business a year ago as a business consultant/coach. After many years working in the city for corporate clients, she felt she could help smaller business owners, work less hours and work on her own terms more.

Her income in the first year was slow to get started but is beginning to see progress with a regular amount of client bookings each month, creating a regular cash flow. She manages all her money in one bank account and struggles to see what actual spare cash she has each month. Therefore, knowing what she can spend on herself or spend on her business is impossible.

Charmayne wants to develop her business online, creating a passive income with online courses and is looking at writing her first book, giving her creditability but also an additional revenue.

Thoughts to consider:

Charmayne needs to open a separate business or sole trader account for all her business revenue to go into. She needs to create a list of outgoings which apply to that account and allow for any annual or future costs she foresees paying, such as marketing. Separately, we would usually suggest Charmayne lists her personal outgoings also, giving a monthly total. Ideally, the two totals should be the initial goal for invoicing clients each month. Ensuring she is strict with terms and conditions for payment i.e.: pay within 14 days or the end of the month, thus giving her three working weeks ahead to have the money in the account. Working with her money ahead of herself will allow Charmayne to stress less about her money and focus more on clients. When the money hits the account, Charmayne should pay herself FIRST, before anyone or anything else. Eventually, as she creates more clients, she can increase the amount she is paying herself.

Having a book keeper or book keeping system linked to her bank accounts will allow her to manage her money more easily and establish a better understanding of what money is hers to spend or invest.

---

More women are becoming entrepreneurs. We're choosing to create a legacy from our hard work, not just settle for earning a living.

Women entrepreneurs can be any age. You may be right out of university, you may have an MBA, professional qualifications or simply be brilliant at what you do.

Our clients are women in their forties and fifties who want to explore a different career and found their passion.

To be a female entrepreneur means becoming someone who is discovering your ability of endurance and developing the crucial belief system on your way to success.

**So here's my advice if you are starting out as an entrepreneur.** Get your concept right, from initial sales and testing. Know what you can charge and make sure you possess sufficient confidence to not be overshadowed or underappreciated by anyone.

Running your own business is a journey of self-discovery. You may have heard that from other people, or read it. Well, it isn't a cliché, it's true. And that means you need someone, such as Evolution for Women, to advise you on your own money.

---

**The fourth stage is the Working Adult or Parent stage 35 years to 54 years.**

This stage is seen as your later working years. It is characterised by the fact that you may have more than one child, your children may be at school and you may be caring for elderly parents.

The financial challenges at this stage of life are more complicated as you may want to help your children pay for their university fees or assist them with a deposit on their first property. Both of these are sizable expenditures so it is worth planning for these as early as you can to build up a decent amount of money by the time it is needed. Again, if you have more than one child, there should be a pot for each.

This is also the time when you need to think about protecting your income in case of injury or illness. A health issue could knock your lifetime savings if you don't have cover and you may not be able to pay the mortgage or the bills. This could have devastating effects on your family and home. It is this stage where most claims are made. According to a report by Legal & General, the average age for critical illness claims is 45 years old and the average age for terminal illness claims is 55 years.

It is worth looking at and revising your pension now. You need to understand how much money you will need for your retirement and the number of years that you can work is reducing, so it is crucial that you can put as much as you can into your pension now.

This is also a time where people re-evaluate their careers or decide that they want to retrain. There is a requirement for more income as the family has more financial needs. Re-training has both cost and time obligations so it is worth having some savings in the pot before you quit your full-time job.

It is also at this stage where a lot of people are caring for their parents, whether it is just their finances or whether they have to move them into a home. There are financial obligations to be met here and it is worth getting sound financial advice in order to maximise assets and ensure that healthcare needs are met.

### Returning to work – Meet Suzie

Suzie has been a stay at home mum for 15 years, previously she worked in a school as an office manager. Now her children are older and don't need her around so much, she is wanting to work 25 hours a week to give herself more spare money each month and to pay for bigger holidays for the family.

All the family's income goes into a joint account with her partner, however, she wants to keep this income separate and pay for some of the bills.

Suzie is unsure what she should be considering financially at this stage of life.

<u>Thoughts to consider</u>

A suggestion would be for Suzie to work out her total net income (so what she would be paid each month into her bank account) and what her partner's net income is. Add up all the key family outgoings. For example: Her income is £850 and her partner is £1850. The outgoings are £1200 per month. She earns 45% of what her partner earns (£850 divided by £1850). Therefore if it was to be equal, he would pay 55% of the outgoings and she would pay 45% (Suzie pays £540 and her partner pays £660). Thus meaning she is contributing an equal proportion based her their income levels.

Depending on how her partner feels about this level of income from her, they may decide to focus her salary on just saving for the family holidays. We would normally suggest the holiday package is priced up and divided by the number of months before the bill needs to be paid, thus giving you a monthly amount to put aside.

However, Suzie also needs to consider her pension options as she hasn't been contributing to one for 15 years and needs to think about what her retirement plans would be once she and her partner retire.

---

Returning to work is a personal issue for us all. Many mums would love to stay home but it's not financially feasible for everyone to do so. Others simply don't want to stay at home for various reasons.

If you have a successful career and you are getting ready to return to work after pregnancy, the first thing to understand is there is never a perfect time. Just like when you started your family in the first place, there is never a 'right' time to go back.

Putting aside the financial benefits of returning and the impact of being off, returning to work is a big emotional step. *I know this from my own experience.*

**So here's my advice.** You need to take control of the situation. Every phase of your life can be controlled by you when you create space for yourself. The space comes from developing the skills, mentality and financial independence.

Communication about money in relationships can be a formidable issue.

Now is the time to talk about the financial goals you and your partner share. Discussing what is important in life involves your budget: debts, cash management, emergency funds, insurance protection, retirement savings and more.

Having a double income contributing to the family home can make things seem rosy, but it all changes when childcare costs come along. It means an added risk if one of you loses your job or becomes ill. Establish what needs to be covered in an emergency and build your plan.

**The fifth stage is the Pre-retirement stage 55 years to 64 years**

You are heading towards retirement, so what do people in this stage need to think about?

A review of your pension is a must. You have less years to work and, therefore, less years to save for your retirement. You need to look at what income you will have for your retirement years and whether you will have enough to last you.

It is worth looking at what you have in savings and investments at this point and seeing if you are able to make more out of them in the next 10 years before you retire. It may be that you need to, or wish to, carry on working after you retire from your current career and do some part-time work or voluntary work to keep you active.

You may want to help your children with their first home or wedding costs, however these are very large purchases and you may need to dip into your savings or other assets in order to help them out. Is this going to affect their inheritance or your lifestyle when you retire?

You may want to re-evaluate your property and whether it is too big for your needs or whether you wish to be closer to your children, or even emigrate. You may be able to save money by downsizing or living somewhere less expensive. Also, take into account that a smaller home will come with cheaper energy bills and lower council tax.

However, if you don't want to move because you are already close to your children and you have them to stay, there are equity release schemes available. Most schemes allow you to borrow money using your home as the security. In essence, you are lending some of your home's value to a company and the scheme will get their money back when your house is sold, more often than not at your death, or if you go into a nursing home.

There are different types of equity release schemes and it is worth researching them before you make your decision. Remember, you will be reducing the amount that you will be leaving to your family in your

Will and such schemes can be expensive to buy. Talk to a financial adviser to make sure that you have looked at all the implications that doing this may have on your financial circumstances.

It is important to make sure that your Will is still valid and relevant. A review is always a great idea as there may be grandchildren who you did not have when you wrote it. You may have decided to help one child out financially and want to leave more of your remaining assets to the other(s) to compensate. But if it's not written down, it may not be sorted out that way once you are gone, so it is better to get it done now.

Whatever you decide to do, make sure you: seek advice; can pay back any money you may borrow; and you are not giving your children a debt that they cannot repay once you have gone.

---

## Empty Nest

I often think there is no starker contrast between my generation and my mother's than when it is time for our children to leave home.

My friends and I, if we didn't go to university, left home in our early twenties, as early as possible for some of my friends. Yet today, for various financial reasons, children are leaving home much later and are likely to return home after university.

When it does happen, it is an emotional event, just like returning to work for the first time. Some of my clients tell me that they didn't know whether to jump up and down with excitement or curl up into a ball and cry.

When your children were at home, your life probably revolved around them. Even older children require practical and emotional support. Now your life is entering a new phase. It's time for you to become an empty nester.

**So here's my advice.** Following some reflection, start planning. Every phase of your life can be controlled by you when you see the possibilities. The possibility to do what you want comes from developing the skills, mentality and financial independence.

Permit yourself to turn your spare cash into savings that can work for you in retirement.

Investing may seem scary and you probably want to make sure you have enough in case anything goes wrong. Well, you can probably protect yourself and still save for your future, it is a case of creating a financial plan that enables you to do both.

The truth is that you can afford to focus on you now. It's your time.

---

## Getting divorced

Meet Deborah, she has been married for 21 years and has recently filed for divorce, her ex-partner and herself have two children aged 12 and 14. She has met with her lawyer but is really at the start of the process and is unsure what will happen and what needs to be looked at. Her partner has dealt with the main finances, however, she looked after day-to-day shopping. She feels ready to understand her new financial future and get into a new strong position.

She plans to continue working part time at the local primary school and wants to retain the family home, so her children do not have to move schools. However, she won't be able to maintain the property or the mortgage on her own with her salary. This is her primary concern.

Thoughts to consider:
The first thing for Deborah to do would be to ensure she has collected as much paperwork as possible. Her lawyer will need to understand all

her debts, assets, income and outgoings at the current property. Her ex-partner will need to do the same for negotiations to start.

Mortgage wise, the lender will take into consideration benefits and court maintenance so Deborah should get a mortgage capacity letter from a broker or mortgage provider to show her lawyer the affordable mortgage options available to her.

The valuation of the property and any assets, such as pensions, are taken into account when it comes to maintenance, short or long term. It is key that Deborah puts herself in a good position so that the mortgage is covered as well as her bills and day-to-day living costs.

---

No one plans to get divorced when they get married but it still happens to around 42% of couples in the UK, according to the Office for National Statistics. And that number may be rising.

Even if you have seen it coming for some time, it's normal to feel numb. Working through the practicalities that your decision involves, can feel overwhelming.

You may be feeling powerless and angry about what has happened if you had not wanted the relationship to end. Compounded with a sense of loss and sadness.

This is a time when you need to get the support and advice of other people. You might also find it helpful to write down all the things you've got to deal with. Now your life is entering a new phase.

**So here's my advice.** Take some time for yourself, by the time the whole process is complete you will be feeling warn out. You might have had to change jobs or houses and your financial position would have most definitely have changed. Following some reflection, you should consider what you want to do next. Every phase of your life can be controlled by you when you see the possibilities. The possibility to do what you want comes from developing the skills, mentality and financial independence. You may want to think about a new career or take up several new hobbies. The truth is that you can afford to focus on you now. It's your time. Depending on where this leaves you, will dictate your next financial plan.

---

**The sixth and last stage is the Retired stage 65-plus years**
Scottish Widows report found that 71% of women don't know what pension pot they need to secure a retirement income they hope for . . . and that 52% of women are saving adequately for retirement.

If you haven't already, this is the time that most people think about downsizing, moving closer to their children or other family members or even emigrating. Depending on your retirement income and your health, it is worth working out how much you have in the pot and what you will need annually to give you the lifestyle that you would like.

It is worth looking at your insurances as they rise quickly once you retire and you may not have adequate cover for your needs. Re-evaluate what you need them for and whether the plans you have in place are relevant to you now. It is worth seeking advice to make sure that you are covered correctly. Also ensure that your Will is up to date and relevant as your situation or that of your children may have changed.

This is the time while you are still fit and healthy and of sound mind, to speak to an adviser and your family to arrange a Lasting Power of Attorney (LPA) for your financial affairs. It will allow someone you trust to look after your assets if you should become too unwell to handle this. You can also do this for health decisions so that someone can talk to your doctor on your behalf. If you haven't put this in place, your family may have to go to court to be granted this power to help you, otherwise your family will have no control over where you should receive your care and how it is funded. You can find more information about this here:

www.gov.uk/government/organisations/office-of-the-public-guardian

Lastly, make sure that you are claiming all the state benefits that you may be entitled to. There are many people who think they do not qualify and are missing out on that useful extra cash at this time in their lives.

**Retiring – meet Mary:**

Mary has paid into a few different company pensions for many years, she is 50 and wishes to retire at age 65. She earns £27,500 per year as a researcher for a charity. She contributes 5% of her salary currently (£114 per month) and her employer matches it. This could mean her pension pot at age 65 would be £151,865. At age 65, she would be able to draw a cash-free lump sum of up to 25% (£37,996) with the remaining funds providing an income of £5,722 per year - £476 per month. Most people would like to see a retirement income of at least around 70% of their current annual salary to live a comfortable lifestyle. In this example, she would be £690 a month short of this.

Her state pension wouldn't start until age 67 and is currently £155.65 per week.

Work out your pensionable income here:
https://www.moneyadviceservice.org.uk/en/tools/pension-calculator

---

We're all living longer, especially women. That means you'll most likely have more time to enjoy your retirement.

Living longer means you have a greater chance of outliving whatever you have saved. In fact, this is often considered the number one financial worry for most women.

To compound it, while my peers and my daughter's generation in particular, have benefitted from gender equality, you are still at a disadvantage when it comes to accumulating money for your retirement. The reality is that you will need to save more to live comfortably in retirement.

**So here's my advice.** Don't enter this phase of your life without any options. Have the skills, have the mentality, and have the financial independence for a long and contented retirement. I'll help you have them and keep them.

Consider how you can turn as much of your spare cash into savings that can work for you in retirement.

Investing may seem risky and you probably want to make sure you have enough for a rainy day. Creating a financial plan enables you to do both. Protect yourself and still secure your future savings.

This has given you snapshots of the various stages in your life with regards to your finances. I would like to think it has helped provide a valuable insight into what financial products you need to set up at certain times in order to make life run that bit more smoothly as you get older. By looking at the life cycle process, you will be able to re-evaluate your plans over time to ensure that you have the correct savings, insurance, investments at each stage, and you will be able to minimise your spending and control your debt to help yourself live the life that you really want.

---

# CHAPTER 12
## Summary

Dear Reader,

Congratulations for reading all the way to the end. I love to read but know myself with family and work commitments often, even with best intentions, I just don't manage it.

I started writing this book with the intention to provide a platform for women to start to understand money wherever they were in their journey. If I have helped one person, it was a success. As I began to realise the task I had taken on, I wanted to achieve more than that and would like to help 5,000 women in the next year. I know the impact that will not only have on them but their families, along with their children's future, and will create a ripple effect that I will never see.

With all the ideas, education and information out there, it is easy to get overwhelmed. I would just ask that you take at least one action a month and stick with it. Then, take a step back and try another. Bit by bit, you can achieve so much. Procrastination and delaying making decisions will not help you to move forward. Baby steps in a year can achieve amazing things.

So in quick summary:

Review where you are now and what your money blocks are

1. Establish which kind of money profile you are

2. Try out the Money Makeover Programme either via this book or using the Evolution for Women online programme

3. Download the Evolution for Women budget planner

4. Use a savings challenge

5.  Evaluate where are you in your money matrix

6.  Download our financial check-list

7.  Download your own money manage software tool

8.  Consider what your next financial milestone is

9.  Make a plan and follow it through


We are certainly here to help and welcome you to join our Facebook group/community where we share up to date blogs and challenges.

Search – 'Evolution for Women - Financial Planning for Women'

You can, of course, keep up to date with us via our newsletter, within which we also share up-to-date news and recent blogs. You just need to go to the Evolution for Women home page to register your email address.

www.evolutionforwomen.co.uk

Alternatively, we hope you will connect with us online via any of the different social media platforms. Wishing you great financial success at whatever level or place that might be.

Best Wishes

# CHAPTER 13
## About the author

Rebecca Robertson CeMAP & DipFA is the multi award-winning founder and director of the financial planning group Evolution for Women. She is a regular media commentator on financial planning and has trained more than 35 new advisers to the industry. With 16 years' experience, she has helped hundreds of clients with their financial needs and is proud to have a 100% satisfaction record from clients.

Rebecca is known as the Independent Financial Adviser who is passionate about putting women firmly in control of their finances. She helps families to achieve financial freedom and gives them peace of mind in knowing their finances are properly protected in the event of the worst happening.

She provides holistic and independent advice to clients, but also gives vital financial planning advice as a media commentator, with regular interviews on BBC Radio Kent and within the Mortgage Introducer magazine, advising on financial issues particularly in relation to women. Rebecca has also appeared in the Independent newspaper's Women in Finance section and is a financial expert for the Talented Ladies Club. She has won financial and banking awards for her work with women's finances.

Rebecca has also grown a women-in-business social enterprise called Evo Girls. This is a way to support and assist business owners grow their companies more quickly than they would alone. She has a vision to run her company nationally. This passion for developing a social enterprise comes from her own business experience and, after making her own mistakes, her realisation that there were a lot of bad practices 'selling' within the sector.

# Colleague Testimonials

I have worked with Rebecca Robertson for more than 10 years initially as colleagues within the mortgage industry and for the past 3 years as business partners.

Rebecca is an extremely experienced finance professional having worked across a wide cross section of the industry in many capacities. She is an excellent financial adviser who is most notably passionate about helping women and families with their finance. All too often in our industry, people target the wealthy high earners who more often than not are still stereo typically male. Rebecca's energy for providing accessible plain English advice to the average family, where the woman is often the main decision maker or influencer, is in my opinion a game changer, hence my joining of Evolution for Women. We do what we do well and with our heads held high as the ethics of the business are so strong and Rebecca created that. Something our industry needs more of.

Rebecca also cares massively about recruiting more women in to financial services. She has had a huge impact on my career and I wouldn't have been able to build at the speed that I have without her coaching, mentoring, support and advice. I'm sure others within the business would say the same.

**Sarah Drakard, Independent Financial Adviser, Evolution for Women**

I love her passion and her direct approach to business. She is tenacious and leads by example . . . not some of the time but all of the time. She is knowledgeable and experienced in the mortgage and protection market. She is not afraid of failure and is totally positive in outlook. Her drive establishes enthusiasm in all who work with her. She does not suffer fools gladly which can be her greatest weakness – but could in some circumstances be her greatest asset. She can be relied upon to deliver her best at every level regardless of the environment she finds herself in. She is fearless in her ambition and I hold her in high esteem. I have the greatest respect for her and her mission and know I can depend upon her. She is one of those people who I could call if I was stuck on the other side of the world in a dire situation.

**Mark Hobbs, Managing Director of New Leaf Distribution**

# Client Testimonials

My husband would claim to be in control of our finances but is terribly disorganised. Finding Evolution for Women & the Good Parent Portfolio has been a godsend. We've saved ourselves a good chunk of cash each month, but best of all I now have the peace of mind that our small children will be provided for should the worst happen. I still have a disorganised husband, but I feel much more in control of things now – Deb

Rebecca looked at my finances and recommended a solution to give us more disposable income but still paying off our mortgage. She made everything clear and the process was quick and painless. And unlike many financial advisers you can easily get hold of her, and she always calls you back. I have recommended Rebecca to friends – Jane

I met Evolution for Women at a Baby Event and speaking to them face to face and not over the phone was very reassuring. They helped me and my partner with our life insurance policies and if I ever needed financial help again I would certainly use Evolution for Women. Rebecca was my adviser and she was always available in a timely manner and offered relevant advice to mine and my partner's needs. Rebecca is very friendly which helps a lot during the process. I would recommend Evolution for Women to anyone who was looking for advice. 10/10 for Evolution for Women

Rebecca was always up to date with my needs and my family needs. She was very friendly and offered us advice based on my needs. Evolution for Women stood out for me because they did not come across as scary and too intimidating, they were friendly and coming into my home helped me relax. I would most definitely choose Evolution for Women again. The customer service was brilliant and was already to help - Lorna

I knew I needed to do a Will and Evolution for Women helped me do this. Rebecca was always available in a timely manner. She explained clearly what we needed to do and how the process was going to happen; she answered all of our questions. Evolution for Women and Rebecca were always friendly and courteous throughout. Overall I would rate the service EXCELLENT! I am always looking out to see what other services Evolution for Women offer. I would most defiantly recommend Evolution for Women to my friends and family.

Rebecca came out to my home to talk through my Will with me. She answered all of my questions and offered relevant advice. Evolution for Women is an excellent company and I would recommend them to anyone -Paul

Rebecca was brilliant, she went through all of my finances and gave advice based on my needs. She was very friendly and helpful; it really was an excellent service - Sarah

*"The reason why I've been so financially successful is my focus has never, for one minute, been on money"*

*~ Oprah*